Awakening Wonder:

A Classical Guide to TRUTH, GOODNESS & BEAUTY

Stephen R. Turley, PhD

Series Editor: Stephen R. Turley, PhD

Awakening Wonder:
A Classical Guide to Truth, Goodness, and Beauty

Version 1.1

ISBN: 978-1-60051-265-0

Cover & layout by Lenora Riley

Classical Academic Press
515 S. 32nd Street
Camp Hill, PA 17011
www.ClassicalAcademicPress.com

PGP.05.17

The entire object of true education is to make people not merely do the right things, but enjoy the right things—not merely industrious, but to love industry—not merely learned, but to love knowledge—not merely pure, but to love purity—not merely just, but to hunger and thirst after justice.

—John Ruskin, *The Crown of Wild Olive: Three Lectures on Work, Traffic, and War*

TABLE OF CONTENTS

INTRODUCTION

> [I]f the too obvious, so straight branches of Truth and Good are crushed or amputated and cannot reach the light—yet perhaps the whimsical, unpredictable, unexpected branches of Beauty will make their way through and soar up *to that very place* and in this way perform the work of all three. And in that case it was not a slip of the tongue for Dostoevsky to say that "Beauty will save the world," but a prophecy.
>
> —Aleksandr Solzhenitsyn, "Beauty Will Save the World: The Nobel Lecture on Literature"

Resounding at the height of the Cold War, Aleksandr Solzhenitsyn's words served as an invitation to the world order of his day to reconsider the nature of reality in a way radically different from the coercion and manipulation inherent in political power. These words were a summons for the Soviet East and the democratic West to remember an identity that both civilizations once shared but that had in the course of the twentieth century been eclipsed by secular statism. Solzhenitsyn's speech was a call for the world to return to Beauty, the effulgent or illuminative manifestation of the loveliness, the delectableness, the delightfulness of the True and the Good. For it is here, in the splendor of Beauty, that our ideological abstractions are relativized by a sacramental imagination that lifts us up collectively into an indissoluble union with the divine source of life. This, for Solzhenitsyn, is the redeeming nature of art through which, regardless of the secular eclipse of Truth and Goodness, Beauty still shines for all to see.

That Beauty serves as an invitation is not new. It has long been recognized that the classical Greek term for "Beauty," *kallos*, is related etymologically to the verb *kalein*, "to call." However, if we are to accept such an invitation, then we are going to have to familiarize ourselves with concepts, vocabulary, and frames of reference that have been largely lost underneath the massive secular colossus that constitutes the modern world. The task will not be easy, but the current classical Christian education renewal provides an exciting and promising context for just such a retrieval.

It is within this trajectory of invitation that I have written this guide. It is an invitation to teacher, parent, and student to throw away the current secular nonsense that pervades so much of what passes as education today, and instead to encounter a world filled with awe and wonder, to cultivate a particular human life that embodies Truth, Goodness, and Beauty, which begins at the fountain of worship and flows out into unlimited cultural pursuits that awaken the divinely imparted meaning of the cosmos and thereby voice creation's praise. It is an invitation to cultivate a life of human flourishing, and thus to be a living testimony that Christ is risen and that God's inextinguishable love has in fact broken into our world. It is an invitation for students to discover that they are in fact citizens of a heavenly city, a global Christian civilization, a sacred space where imaginations are sanctified and senses are redeemed that even now celebrates and anticipates the divine renewal of all things.

To this end, I shall develop an extended primer on the conceptual and historical relationship among Truth, Goodness, and Beauty and their shaping of our humanity in a distinctively Christian educational project. Chapter 1 sets the stage with a historical overview of our civilizational context, one that has emptied objective value from our experience of the world and redefined radically the nature of what it means to be human. Chapter 2 takes us back to the historical source of objective values in the classical world, with a focus on the unprecedented contribution of Plato to the development of the divine nature of the True, the Good, and the Beautiful and the educational project by which such values are imparted to students. Chapters 3 and 4 survey the Christian recalibration of these values around the Incarnation of Christ and the revelation of the Trinity in the formative period of Christian orthodoxy, as represented by key contributors from both the Greek East and the Latin West. Chapter 5 examines the subjective appropriation of Truth, Goodness, and Beauty in the Christian development of what we shall call the "redemption of the senses." Chapter 6 explores the significance of Truth, Goodness, and Beauty in the consecration of the imagination in what we shall call the "moral imagination." Finally, chapter 7 outlines a number of aesthetic suggestions for the teaching of Truth, Goodness, and Beauty in such a way that awakens wonder and awe in the imaginations of student and teacher alike.

And so let us together answer this invitation, one that calls all of us to a particular kind of life, a life of true and flourishing humanity in the midst of a cosmos redeemed in Christ, a journey that makes its way through and soars up to that light by which we see light.

Chapter One
A Tale of Two Civilizations

Waterfalls and the World

In 1944 a book critiquing the state of British education was published, titled *The Abolition of Man*. The author was C. S. Lewis. His critique was initiated by a textbook, which he leaves unnamed, calling it *The Green Book*, written by two authors he also leaves unnamed, referring to them as Gaius and Titius. The authors of this book recount poet Samuel Taylor Coleridge's famous visit to the Falls of the Clyde in Scotland in the early 1800s. As Coleridge stood before the waterfall, he overheard the responses of two tourists: one remarked that the waterfall was "sublime," while the other said it was "pretty." Coleridge mentally endorsed the first judgment and rejected the second with disgust. Gaius and Titius then offer their own commentary on this scene:

> When the man said *That is sublime*, he appeared to be making a remark about the waterfall. . . . Actually . . . he was not making a remark about the waterfall, but a remark about his own feelings. What he was saying was really *I have feelings associated in my mind with the word "Sublime,"* or shortly, *I have sublime feelings*. . . . This confusion is continually present in language as we use it. We appear to be saying something very important about something: and actually we are only saying something about our own feelings.[1]

1. C. S. Lewis, *The Abolition of Man or Reflections on Education with Special Reference to the Teaching of English in the Upper Forms of Schools* (New York: Harper & Row, 1971), 2.

For Lewis, this comment by Gaius and Titius had nothing less than cosmic consequences. The waterfall scene and the commentary captured, in microcosmic fashion, *two contrasting conceptions of the world*: one, represented by Samuel Taylor Coleridge, that affirmed Beauty as an objective value embedded in a created cosmic order and recognized by a humanity that participates in that cosmic order; the other, represented by Gaius and Titius and *The Green Book*, that denied objective value in impersonal nature and located all conceptions of Beauty and sublimity to the human mind and to personal preference. In the former, Beauty is a value that exists objective to the knower and in which the knower participates by virtue of his createdness; in the latter, Beauty is a value constructed by the knower and superimposed on an impersonal world. For Lewis, these two perspectives represent nothing less than two fundamentally different human projects constituting two fundamentally different ages or civilizations: what we might call the *moral* age versus the *modern* age, or the *sapient* age versus the *scientific* age.

Cosmic Piety

The key problem that Lewis was trying to diagnose for the reader is that the collapse of Truth, Goodness, and Beauty into subjective processes and private preferences is inextricably linked to the collapse of meaning in the modern age. Just a cursory survey of classic literary texts from cultures all over the world demonstrates that humanity once shared the perspective that the world in which we live was very much brimming with divine life. This diaphanous world eventually formed a particular kind of social orientation and disposition, what classical scholars André-Jean Festugière and Jean Pépin call "cosmic piety," which was nearly universal in the Greco-Roman world. For the Greeks, there was a profound sense that one was truly human only to the extent that one lived in a harmonious relationship with the cosmos.[2] This piety entailed that every person born into the world was born with a divine obligation; we were all born into a morally defined cosmic order and were thus obliged to live in a way concomitant with that moral order.

Truth, Goodness, and Beauty were not merely subjective preferences or private opinions but rather three distinct yet interrelated manifestations of the divine reality of the cosmos.

It is from this world, particularly the Greek world, that our conceptions of the True, the Good, and the Beautiful emerged. Truth, Goodness, and Beauty were not merely subjective preferences or private opinions but rather three distinct yet interrelated manifestations of the divine reality of the cosmos.[3] It was believed that by embodying the True, Good, and Beautiful through the Greek educational project known as *paideia*, students cultivated a virtuous balance in their souls that reflected the balance of the cosmos. Having achieved such balance, students were thereby prepared to take their place in the *polis*, the Greek city-state, which served ideally as the substantiation of cosmic piety. Thus, everything involved in the culture of the *polis*—history, art, music, literature, economics, science, mathematics, politics—served as a palpable, substantial,

---

2. André-Jean Festugière, *Le Dieu Cosmique*, vol. II of *La Révélation D'Hermès Trismégiste* (Paris: Librairie Lecoffre, 1949); idem, *Personal Religion among the Greeks* (Berkeley: University of California Press, 1954), 105–142; Jean Pépin, "Cosmic Piety," in A. H. Armstrong and A. A. Armstrong, eds., *Classical Mediterranean Spirituality: Egyptian, Greek, Roman*, vol. 15 of *World Spirituality* (New York: Crossroads, 1986), 408–435.
3. It should be noted that while the terms *Truth*, *Goodness*, and *Beauty* are often associated with the classical world, their initial systematic treatments are not until the eighteenth century. Thus, the term complex is being used here and throughout the book as a heuristic tool to help illuminate the metaphysical, ethical, and aesthetic constituents distinctive of a classical and Christian engagement with the world. See the discussion in Alister E. McGrath, *The Open Secret: A New Vision for Natural Theology* (Oxford: Blackwell Publishing, 2008), 221–231. Cf. the statement by Victor Cousin, *Lectures on the true, the beautiful, and the good*, translated by O. W. Wight (New York: D. Appleton & Co., 1861), 34: "Philosophy, in all times, turns upon the fundamental ideas of the true, the beautiful, and the good."

and material embodiment of the divine meaning or purpose infused into the world, enabling the human soul to flourish.

With the emergence of Christian civilization, Christians tapped into this cosmic piety, but they also radically altered it. Christians certainly affirm that all people are born into a world of divine obligation; however, they introduce something wholly new by transferring this cosmic piety away from the planets and celestials spheres and imputing it onto Christ, who is the *Logos*, the new creation, in whom all things hold together and through whom God is revealed as the infinite fountain of Trinitarian love and delight. And it is the church, the *ekklesia*, that fulfills this divine obligation by reconstituting time and space around Christ through Word and sacrament, thus enabling us to fulfill our divine purpose and thereby become truly human.

Splitting the World Apart

However, with the advent of the modern age, and more specifically the advancement of modern science, knowledge has become increasingly redefined in such a way so as to exclude any divine moral order. With the breakup of Christendom and the subsequent secularization of the university in the sixteenth and seventeenth centuries, it became increasingly plausible to view knowledge as limited solely to what could be verified by a *method*, namely, the application of science and mathematics. It was argued that only those things that could be verified by the empirical method could be known in a way completely detached from the preconceptions of the observer. Anything that was not subjected to or failed this method was reduced to the state of person-relativity and excluded from the arena of what can be known. But there was a toll that had to be paid for this new knowledge: we collectively had to surrender the concept of meaning or purpose as a reality divinely embedded in a created order, since meaning was impervious to method; *telos* simply could not be placed in a test tube.

Thus, this new conception of knowledge in effect exposed all value systems as mere cultural fabrications. Science has uncovered a world governed not by the gods or any kind of divine meaning but rather by physical, chemical, and biological causal laws. "Objective" values are merely culturally specific meaning systems contrived by humans and imposed on an otherwise meaningless world operated by cause-and-effect processes. Far from an embodiment of divine meaning inherent in a diaphanous cosmos, culture is the collection of mechanisms composed of common symbols, practices, and arrangements shared among a distinct population by which meaning is imputed to an otherwise meaningless world. Modern science has therefore rent asunder what the classical imagination brought together: the physical world and the semiotic world, the world of nature and the world of culture, have been split apart from each other, such that what was once considered knowledge—indeed the highest form of knowledge, the contemplation of the True, the Good, and the Beautiful—is now appropriated as no more than private belief or personal preference.

Christians introduce something wholly new by transferring this cosmic piety away from the planets and celestials spheres and imputing it onto Christ.

And herein lies Lewis's concern with *The Green Book*. If education is enculturation, as the Greeks observed, then *The Green Book* represents nothing less than the attempt to enculturate students into this modern vision of the world, a world known through the lens of empirical verifiability that must *by definition* turn students away from this vision of cosmic piety and cut them off from encountering the cosmic values of Truth, Goodness, and Beauty. Indeed, according to Gaius and Titius and *The Green Book*, the True, the Good, and the Beautiful are now whatever one wants them to be. We are all now born into a world where we have no divine obligations whatsoever apart from what we choose personally to impose on ourselves.

And yet Lewis observed that while moderns have in effect abandoned divine cosmology, the values specific to such a cosmos remain, lingering in our consciences and our expectations. We seem to expect that virtues will be operative in our society all the while rejecting their source. In Lewis's words:

> And all the time—such is the tragic-comedy of our situation—we continue to clamour for those very qualities we are rendering impossible. You can hardly open a periodical without coming across the statement that what our civilization needs is more "drive," or dynamism, or self-sacrifice, or "creativity." In a sort of ghastly simplicity we remove the organ and demand the function. We make men without chests and expect of them virtue and enterprise. We laugh at honour and are shocked to find traitors in our midst. We castrate and bid the geldings be fruitful.[4]

We cannot teach our students that Truth is relative and expect our politicians to be honest; we can't claim that the Good has been replaced by situational ethics and expect our bankers to ground their business decisions in anything other than profit, greed, and expediency; and we cannot relegate Beauty to personal preference and then feign shock when we encounter a urinal as part of an art exhibit.

Lewis recognized profound consequences entailed in modern, value-neutral education. If all values are relegated to the person-relative, if all conceptions of Truth, Goodness, and Beauty are collapsed into the subjective as personal preferences, then the only way there can be a moral consensus in society is through the use of coercion. If a sense of divine obligation and hence self-government has been erased, then only coercion, compulsion, and extortion can provide a motivation

4. Lewis, *Abolition of Man*, 26.

for ethical conformity. Thus, Lewis saw manipulation at the heart of this brave new world to which we are embarking. And if manipulation is an intrinsic characteristic of modern life, then there must surface by definition two classes of people: manipulators and manipulatees, or, in Lewis's terms, the "conditioners" and the "conditioned." The need for coercion and manipulation thus gives rise to the formation of a social elite, a secular aristocracy, with the vast majority of the human population repositioned as objects of manipulation. Thus, Lewis concluded that modern education enculturates students into a world constituted by conditioners and the conditioned, a new social order that subsumes the vast majority of humanity under the category of impersonal Nature, which in effect redefines humanity as inherently meaningless; hence the title of his book, *The Abolition of Man*.

The World Made Whole

Lewis believed that the fate of human nature itself was dependent on our recovery of what he termed the *Tao*, the doctrine of objective values:

> We have been trying, like Lear, to have it both ways: to lay down our human prerogative and yet at the same time to retain it. It is impossible. Either we are rational spirit obliged for ever to obey the absolute values of the *Tao*, or else we are mere nature to be kneaded and cut into new shapes for the pleasures of masters who must, by hypothesis, have no motive but their own "natural" impulses. Only the *Tao* provides a common human law of action which can over-arch rulers and ruled alike. A dogmatic belief in objective value is necessary to the very idea of a rule which is not tyranny or an obedience which is not slavery.[5]

5. Ibid., 73. For an exceptional exploration of the cosmic values in the writings of C. S. Lewis, see Louis Markos, *Restoring Beauty: The Good, the True, and the Beautiful in the Writings of C. S. Lewis* (Colorado Springs: Biblica, 2010).

If there is to be a recovery of Truth, Goodness, and Beauty in our time, the chasm between nature and culture, the physical and the meaningful, will have to be bridged by a rediscovery of cosmic piety. It is my contention that the Incarnation provides just such a bridge, for it is in the Incarnation that we discover a union between the Word and the world, the physical and the semiotic, the natural and the cultural. The Incarnation thus invites us today, in a comparable manner to which it has invited previous generations, to reconsider our cultural memories and metaphysics, what we appropriate as fact and mere fable, what we construct as constituents of public life versus private life, and to encounter the world through a new conception of knowledge, one rooted in the sacramental revelation of the Trinity and the redemption of the human senses. Indeed, it is the Incarnation that beckons us not merely to a new way of knowing our world but to a new way of experiencing and encountering our world as it has been redeemed in Christ and restored proleptically in the shared life-world of the Church.

If a sense of divine obligation and hence self-government has been erased, then only coercion, compulsion, and extortion can provide a motivation for ethical conformity.

However, if we are to return to an Incarnationally informed encounter with Truth, Goodness, and Beauty, we must begin by rediscovering the basic frames of reference by which these cosmic values emerged in the Greco-Roman world and then see their development in the works of key Christian figures in both the Greek East and the Latin West. It is to these frames of reference that we now turn.

Chapter Two
Truth, Goodness, and Beauty in the Classical World

Introduction

In order to appreciate the role of Truth, Goodness, and Beauty in our educational renewal, we have to understand the historical and social context in which these values emerged. This context provides a network of cosmic, anthropological, and social frames of reference that will serve as a model for our exploration of Truth, Goodness, and Beauty throughout our discussion.

Cosmic Piety, the Human Person, and the *Polis*

At the dawning of the first century, nearly universal throughout the Greco-Roman world was what we have called "cosmic piety," the idea that the world is very much brimming with divine life. Because the cosmos is divine, every person is born into a world of divine obligation, such that one is obliged to conform one's life into a harmonious relationship with the world and humanity. At the heart of this cosmology is the micro-macro relationship between the human body and the cosmos, in which the individual human person is a microcosmic replication, literally a *mikros kosmos*, of the substance and order of the macrocosmic world. Reciprocally, the cosmos is seen as a *macro-anthropos*, a cosmic human. This micro-macro relationship originated with pre-Socratic philosophers, particularly Empedocles (490–430 BC), who is credited with being the first to systematize the four cosmic elements (earth, air, fire, water) with the four humors of the human body (black bile, yellow bile, phlegm, and blood).[1] Empedocles argued that the humors play a role in the human body analogous to that played by the elements in the world at large. In fact, classical medical theory as found in Alcmaeon, the Hippocratic corpus, Celsus, and Galen is based precisely on this micro-individual/macro-cosmic relationship, so that sickness or disease is considered an imbalance—a disorder—of the four humors, with health achieved by restoring balance—or symmetry—to the human body reflective of the symmetry of the cosmos.

Eventually, the *polis* or Greek city-state came to be seen as the integrative bridge between the microcosmic human person and the macrocosmic world. From Anaximander (611–546 BC) onward, a rhetorical motif developed that likened the city-state to the human body, such that the city was the individual "writ large"; the city in turn could be viewed as a microcosm, and the cosmos as a city.[2] The cosmic significance of the city-state was most explicit in the temples, which were considered architectural models of the cosmos. According to Dio Cassius, the magnificent cupola of the Pantheon was modeled after the heavens.[3] Isidore of Seville similarly observed: "The Ancients used to make the roofs of their temples in the form of a tortoise shell; so as to represent the sky, which they could see was curved."[4] The third-century Neo-Platonist Porphyry described the mithraeum as "a model of the universe," a miniature replica of the cosmos.[5]

1. James Longrigg, *Greek Rational Medicine: Philosophy and Medicine from Alcmaeon to the Alexandrians* (London: Routledge, 1993), 53.
2. M. R. Wright, *Cosmology in Antiquity* (New York: Routledge, 1995), 71.
3. Dio Cassius, *Roman History Vol. VI,* ed. and trans. by Earnest Cary. Loeb Classical Library. (Cambridge: Harvard University Press, 1980), 53.27.2.
4. Isidore of Seville, *Etymologies*, trans. Stephen A Barney et al (Cambridge: Cambridge University Press, 2006), 15.8.8.
5. Roger Beck, *The Religion of the Mithras Cult in the Roman Empire: Mysteries of the Unconquered Sun* (Oxford: Oxford University Press, 2006), 41, quoted from Porphyry, *De antro nympharum* 6.

These cosmic, anthropological, and civic frames of reference converged into the conception of a cosmic *koinonia* or communion. Plato (427–347 BC) illustrated this notion when he observed that *koinonia* is the basis for the preservation of the whole cosmos, such that "heaven and earth and gods and men are held together by communion and friendship."[6] Sacrifices and divination ceremonies are thus for the purpose of "communion between gods and men."[7] The city-state thus transforms into a cosmopolis. As particularly evident in Plato's *Republic*, the cosmopolis was envisioned as conjoining and creating a harmony among the cosmos, human soul, and society.

These cosmic, anthropological, and civic frames of reference converged into the conception of a cosmic koinonia or communion.

This value that the Greeks placed on cosmic communion, a harmonious relationship between gods and men that perpetuated the vital life processes that sustained the world, gave rise to a distinct education project known as *paideia*. Flourishing in the fourth century BC, *paideia* had as its purpose the formation of a particular kind of human, one in which the heroic virtues, the *arête*—embedded particularly in the texts of Homer and Hesiod—were embodied in the hearts and the minds of students.[8] The idea was that through embodying or imitating the virtues characteristic of cosmic piety, students would transform into citizens of the *polis* who could perpetuate this cosmic communion and realize human flourishing.

---

6. F. Hauck, "κοινός, κοινωνός, κοινωνέω, κοινωνία, συγκοινωνός, συγκοινενέω, κοινωνικός, κοινόω," in Gerhard Kittel et al., eds., *Theological Dictionary of the New Testament*, trans. Geoffrey W. Bromiley (Grand Rapids: Eerdmans, 1977), 3:799, quoted from Plato, *Gorgias* 507e, 508a.
7. Plato, *Symposium* 188b–c, in *Plato in Twelve Volumes*, vol. 9, trans. Harold N. Fowler (Cambridge, MA: Harvard University Press, 1925).
8. Werner Jaeger, *Paideia: The Ideals of Greek Culture*, 3 vols. (New York: Oxford University Press, 1944).

The True, the Good, and the Beautiful

It is in this civilizational context that we first encounter the emergence of the cosmic values known as the True, the Good, and the Beautiful. The Greek term *aletheia* ("truth") literally means "nonconcealment," the negation of *lethein*, "to elude notice, to be unseen."[9] *Aletheia* thus connotes a sense of disclosure: "*truth* in the sense of the *unhiddenness* . . . and *disclosedness* of the state of affairs which exhibits itself and is therefore perceived in its actuality."[10] The term *agathos* ("good") as an adjective connoted "the significance or excellence of a thing or person" and was eventually developed by philosophers to designate the goal, purpose, or meaning of existence.[11] Likewise, *kalos* ("beauty") is generally rendered as "beautiful," "healthy," "excellent," "strong," or "good."[12] It is during the fifth century BC that we find two of the three terms used together. For example, *kalos* is first used together with *agathos* in a political or social context: the *kaloi* and *agathoi* are leading citizens who embody the virtues of the *polis*, the Greek city-state. Indeed, the synonymity of the terms contracted into a single word, *kalokagathia*.

Plato and the "Socratic Trinity"

However, it is not until the writings of Plato that these three terms converge into mutually interpreting concepts, in what has

9. Christopher P. Long, *Aristotle on the Nature of Truth* (Cambridge: Cambridge University Press, 2010), 26.
10. H. Hübner, "ἀλήθεια," in Horst Balz et al, eds., *Exegetical Dictionary of the New Testament* (Grand Rapids: Eerdmans, 1993), 1:57–60, 58.
11. Walter Grundmann, "ἀγαθός," in *Theological Dictionary of the New Testament*, 1:10–17, 10–11.
12. Georg Bertram, "καλός," in *Theological Dictionary of the New Testament*, 3:536–556.

been termed the "Socratic trinity" or "Platonic triad." Though Plato did not provide a systematic treatment of Truth, Goodness, and Beauty, it is not coincidental that the first clear presentation of the True, the Good, and the Beautiful historically comes from a fifteenth-century commentary on Plato's *Philebus* by the Italian humanist scholar Marsilio Ficino.[13]

Truth, Goodness, and Beauty for Plato were divine concepts; they make up what he called the *eidon*, the eternal transcendent world of the ideas or forms. This Socratic trinity is the eternal source of life in which the totality of our cosmos participates as an *eikon*, a temporal, finite image or icon of the eternal transcendent world of the Ideas or Forms. For Plato, the universe is very much alive, or at least inextricably bound up with divine activity, and is thereby considered an object of veneration. In the *Timaeus*, the world is animated by a rational soul, which is the macrocosmic basis for the microcosmic human soul.[14] Humans, as microcosmic replications of the larger macrocosmic world, are composed of tripartite souls that loosely correspond to the Socratic trinity: *logos*, *thymos* or *ethos*, and *eros* or *epithymetes*. The *logos* involves our rational capacities; the *thymos* or *ethos* involves our emotional, ethical, or moral capacities; and the *epithymetes* or *eros* involves our desires and aesthetic capacities.[15] And it is through the tripartite soul that was forged in the world of the forms before our birth and embodiment (Plato held more or less to a doctrine of reincarnation) that the individual human can mirror, reflect, or image the virtues of the True, the Good, and the Beautiful, and thus exemplify and participate in divine life.

Now, for Plato, the dilemma is that we as tripartite souls already possess a knowledge of the virtues, literally the divine order of the

13. Marsilio Ficino, *The Philebus Commentary*, trans. Michael J. B. Allen (Berkeley: University of California Press, 1975), 78, 110. On the development of Truth, Goodness, and Beauty as a Romantic response to the reductionist rationalism of the eighteenth and nineteenth centuries, see Alister E. McGrath, *The Open Secret*, 221–231.
14. Plato, *Timaeus*, ed. and trans. by R.G. Bury, Loeb Classical Library (Cambridge: Harvard University Press, 1952), 33b, 36e, 41d.
15. Plato, *Republic* 435e8–9, 439e3–4, 439d5–7, in *Plato in Twelve Volumes*, vols. 5 and 6, trans. Paul Shorey (Cambridge, MA: Harvard University Press, 1969).

eternal ideas or forms—the imprint—of the True, the Good, and the Beautiful, but this knowledge has been forgotten as the result of our birth and embodiment. As he made clear in his *Meno*, knowledge does not derive from inductive or deductive processes or an investigation into the nature of things, but rather knowledge is a *recollection*, what Plato termed *anamnesis*, a recovery of Truth insofar as our souls have experienced it prior to our embodiment.[16] So the key here is that knowledge needs to be *awakened*. And it is *philosophia*, the love of wisdom, that seeks to recover human perception of the True, the Good, and the Beautiful so as to restore the human soul to its participation in divine life. This pursuit of Truth in the *Phaedrus* and *Gorgias*, of Goodness in the *Republic*, and of Beauty in Diotima's speech in the *Symposium*, in effect reorients the human person to the divine world of the eternal and immutable, and thereby effects a harmonious relationship with the cosmos, which itself participates in divine life.

The Platonic Conception of Truth, Goodness, and Beauty

The precise relationship between the True, the Good, and the Beautiful in Plato is very difficult to determine, largely because these concepts are not treated systematically but rather are spread out among his works. But we can map out a broad, general model for how they work together in relation to the tripartite soul.

For Plato, the Good is not simply a thing or a value; the Good is universal priority in which all true things participate and from which they exist.

16. Plato, *Meno* 86b. See, e.g., John McGuckin, "The Notion of the Beautiful in Ancient Greek Thought and Its Christian Patristic Transfiguration," *The Voice of Orthodoxy* XIII, no. 5 (September–October 2009), available at www.thevoiceoforthodoxy.com/archives/articles/notion_of_the_beautiful.html.

In book VII of the *Republic*, Plato considered the Good to be the universal principle, the self-sufficient source of all being and the irreducible essence of reality:

> [I]n the region of the known the last thing to be seen and hardly seen is the idea of Good, and that when seen it must needs point us to the conclusion that this is indeed the cause for all things of all that is right and beautiful, giving birth in the visible world to light, and the author of light and itself in the intelligible world being the authentic course of truth and reason.[17]

For Plato, the Good is not simply a thing or a value; the Good is universal priority in which all true things participate and from which they exist. The Good is "beyond being" and is thus the foundation of all hypotheses which requires no hypothesis; that Idea from which all Ideas emerge and on which they depend.[18] According to his allegory of the cave in book VII of the *Republic*, the Good is to the world of Ideas much like what the sun is to our perceptible, physical world. As such, the Good, the divine source of life, is in itself unknowable, being the essence, the light, by which all things are known and perceived. The Good itself must thus be *revealed*; it must be communicated to the human mind by means of *aletheia* or "Truth."[19] Drawing from the allegory of the cave, we might say that Truth is the splendor of the Good that can be perceived by the soul.[20] For Plato, Truth involves understanding how all things in our world, all particulars, participate in and derive their nature from

17. Plato, *Republic* 517b–c, in *Plato in Twelve Volumes,* vols. 5 and 6, trans. Paul Shorey (Cambridge, MA: Harvard University Press, 1969).
18. Ibid., 509b, 510b, 511b, 526e. See Werner Beierwaltes, "The Love of Beauty and the Love of God," in A. H. Armstrong and A. A. Armstrong, eds., *Classical Mediterranean Spirituality: Egyptian, Greek, Roman,* vol. 15 of *World Spirituality* (New York: Crossroads, 1986), 297–298.
19. The precise relationship between the Good and the True in Plato as particularly found in books VI and VII of the *Republic* is the object of considerable scholarly debate. On the various interpretations, see the overview in D. C. Schindler, *Plato's Critique of Impure Reason: On Goodness and Truth in the Republic* (Baltimore: Catholic University of America Press, 2008).
20. Plato, *Republic* 508d.

the Good.[21] Thus, concomitant with its etymology, it is the nature of Truth to *reveal* or *disclose* reality, the priority of the Good, to the human mind or *logos*.

However, the Good is not merely revealed to the mind through Truth. A desire, an *eros*, is awakened for the Good within the human soul through *kalos* or "Beauty." In Diotima's speech in the *Symposium*, Beauty is the object of *eros* or love.[22] And it is here that Plato revealed the means by which the soul encounters the True and the Good. In awakening *eros*, Plato's conception of Beauty becomes inextricably linked with Grecian physics, in that *eros* constitutes the law of attraction. Empedocles had envisioned the cosmos as a whole and all the particulars within it, including humans, as directed by *eros* and *eris*, literally "desire" and "strife," which served as the opposing forces of attraction and repulsion. In accordance with Greco-Roman physics, this love, this desire awakened through Beauty, serves the indispensable role of *momentum* or *motivation* in intellectual, moral, and spiritual pursuits. This is why we associate Beauty with "attraction"; through Beauty we are drawn to the True and the Good. By awakening *eros* within us, Beauty provides us with the allure, the momentum, the gravitational pull toward the True and the Good and thus unites us with the divine source of life:

> When a man has been thus far tutored in the lore of love, passing from view to view of beautiful things, in the right and regular ascent, suddenly he will have revealed to him, as he draws to the close of his dealings in love, a wondrous vision, beautiful in its nature; and this, Socrates, is the final object of all those previous toils. . . . Beginning from obvious beauties he must for the sake of that highest Beauty be ever climbing aloft, as one the rungs of a ladder, from one to two, and from two to all beautiful bodies; from personal Beauty he proceeds to beautiful observances, from observance

21. Ibid., 475e ff.
22. Plato, *Symposium* 210a–d.

> to beautiful learning, and from learning at last to that particular study which is concerned with the beautiful itself and that alone; so that in the end he comes to know the very essence of Beauty.[23]

The important point here is that Beauty, because of its divine nature, is always linked with the True and the Good. In order for something to be truly beautiful, it must by definition draw one to the True and the Good. When *eros* or love is amputated from Truth and Goodness, say in the case of pornography, it is no longer love but rather lust or *epithymia*.[24] The Greeks alluded to this differentiation in the mythologies of the Muses and the Sirens: the Muses are the daughters of Zeus who inspire Beauty and Truth, while the Sirens are water nymphs who lure sailors to their deaths through their bewitching songs. So we see here a highly ethical significance to this encounter with the True, the Good, and the Beautiful. Because Beauty communicates the True and the Good through its radiance, the awakening of *eros* always involves the awakening of *arête*—the classical virtues (wisdom, moderation, justice, and courage)—which occurs when the *logos*, *thymos*, and *epithymetes* or *eros* constituting the tripartite human soul reflect the balance or harmony of the cosmos.[25] Thus Plato saw an inextricable link between virtue and a true knowledge of the world.

The important point here is that Beauty, because of its divine nature, is always linked with the True and the Good. In order for something to be truly beautiful, it must by definition draw one to the True and the Good.

---

23. Plato, *Symposium* 210e-211d, in *Plato in Twelve Volumes,* vol. 9, trans. Harold N. Fowler (Cambridge, MA: Harvard University Press, 1925).
24. Plato, *Republic* 328d; cf. *Laws* 854a; *Phaedrus* 83b.
25. Cf. ibid., 442a.

ENCOUNTERING TRUTH, GOODNESS, AND BEAUTY THROUGH *PAIDEIA*

For Plato, the educational project of *paideia* involves teaching students to repudiate what deserves repudiation and to love what is in fact lovely and deserving of our desires.[26] This involves what amounts to be a three-stage process.

First, there is the need to realize there is in fact a problem, that one is in fact ignorant and incapable of accounting for reality. This admission of personal impoverishment, what the Greeks called *aporia* and the Latins called *pietas*, is the rationale for the Socratic Dialogue; Socrates was able to impart wisdom only when his interlocutor admits ignorance and perplexity.

Second, this intellectual and spiritual vacuousness, this virtue of humility, can then be *filled*—and filled not merely with facts but with a recollection of the knowledge of the world as it relates to that which is eternally True, Good, and Beautiful. This stage involves a twofold purification by which students cultivate a detachment from false things and an attachment to true things. The twofold purification consists of a *moral* and an *intellectual* purification. Moral purification involves the practice of the virtues, which in effect distances the soul from the confines and temptations of the body. Intellectual purification, or *theoria*, involves contemplation of the True, the Good, and the Beautiful, particularly in mathematics, where students are able see the reality that lies beyond appearances. Thus, all subjects in an educational curriculum serve as lenses through which the True, the Good, and the Beautiful can be encountered. Gymnastics cultivate the virtue of *enkrateia* or self-mastery; music and poetry provide the chief means by which the

26. Plato, *Laws,* ed. and trans. by R.G. Bury, Loeb Classical Library (Cambridge: Harvard University Press, 1968), 653b6–c4.

rhythm and harmony of the cosmos can be communicated through the body and sunk deeply into the recesses of the soul.[27]

Third, there is ultimate *theoria*, the union of the soul with the True, the Good, and the Beautiful, a beatific vision that one simply cannot experience while embodied. One experiences this vision only at death.[28]

SUMMARY

Truth, Goodness, and Beauty emerge historically in a world very much removed from our own. This world was characterized by cosmic piety, the sense that the universe was alive with divine presence and thus obligated all people born into the world to live a particular kind of life, one that oriented the self into a harmonious relationship with the world and others. This obligation was lived out in the life of the *polis*, the city-state, which served as the civic center for communion between men and the gods. In order to foster a harmonious relationship with the cosmos and city, the Greek educational project called *paideia* sought to instill within students a love for the cosmic values: Truth, Goodness, and Beauty. As particularly developed in the work of Plato, these values served as the harmonious model for cultivating a comparable harmony in one's own soul, which one then lived out in harmony with one's fellow man, and thus exemplified and perpetuated the cosmic harmony that sustained the world.

The educational project of paideia *involves teaching students to repudiate what deserves repudiation and to love what is in fact lovely and deserving of our desires.*

---

27. Andrew Louth, *The Origins of the Christian Mystical Tradition: From Plato to Denys* (Oxford: Oxford University Press, 1981), 8.
28. Plato, *Phaedo*, ed. and trans. by Harold North Fowler, *Plato,* Vol. I, Loeb Classical Library (Cambridge: Harvard University Press, 1977), 66c–67a.

Plato's philosophy provides us with the cosmic, anthropological, and civic frames of reference for the emergence of a distinctly Christian development of the True, the Good, and the Beautiful, and it is to this Christian reappropriation that we now turn.

Chapter Three
Truth, Goodness, and Beauty in the Christian World, Part I
The Greek East

Introduction

As we discovered in chapter 2, Truth, Goodness, and Beauty are part of a particular conception of the universe, one we called "cosmic piety," in which the universe is considered to be filled with divine meaning and purpose, which obligates all people to live in a particular harmonious way toward the world and their fellow man. At the heart of this cosmic piety are the cosmic values of Truth, Goodness, and Beauty, which bring balance to the human soul and society alike.

In this chapter, I want to explore how the Christian reconceptualization of the cosmos involved a proportionate reappropriation of Truth, Goodness, and Beauty. We will find that Christians do indeed tap into the cosmic, anthropological, and civic frames of reference characteristic of Plato and the classical world, all the while radically altering these frames of reference in ways that forge a vision of Truth, Goodness, and Beauty that is wholly unprecedented. I will begin with the New Testament witness of the re-creation of the world in Christ and then explore the implications of this Christ-centered cosmology for the development of distinctively Christian conceptions of Truth, Goodness, and Beauty.

The New Testament Witness

The prologue of the Gospel of John begins: "In the beginning was the *Logos*, and the *Logos* was with God, and the *Logos* was God." The term *logos* represents one of the central concepts in classical Greek culture. *Logos* has the dual meaning of "counting" and "speaking," and thus from its beginning it had the sense of a linguistic order or metrical word and was associated very much with verbally expressed ratio relations.[1] Starting with Heraclitus in the sixth century BC, the term increasingly began to be associated with the world as a grand rational and intelligible order, what the Greeks called *cosmos*. Many of us are familiar with the Latin-rooted term *quintessence*; in classical cosmology there were four essences—earth, air, fire, and water—and the *quintessence*, or what the Greeks called *logos*, was the cosmic principle in which the totality of the universe cohered.

As evidenced by the Gospel of John, Christians in the Greco-Roman world tap into this idea of an integrated cosmos while at the same radically modifying it. For example, like Heraclitus, Christians affirm a cosmically comprehensive *Logos* but take the unprecedented step of identifying that divine *Logos* as a divine Person who became flesh and dwelt among us (John 1:14). Further, Christians replace an eternal cosmos with creation *ex nihilo,* which in effect overturns the entire Greco-Roman metaphysical order. While the Greco-Roman creation myths were concerned with how the gods brought order out of chaos, the Christian creation account involves a *radical* creation of the cosmos; the Christian God created literally every square inch of the cosmos, such that the operating physics of the cosmos is not power over chaos but rather divine gratuity and love. Indeed, the translators of the Septuagint, the early Greek translation of the Hebrew Scriptures, anticipated this relationship between God's spoken word, his *Logos*, and the nature of creation in its translation of the refrain "and

1. See Eva Brann, *The Logos of Heraclitus* (Philadelphia: Paul Dry Books, 2011).

God saw that it was good." Rather than translate the Hebrew word *tob*, "good," with the Greek equivalent, *agathos*, the translators chose *kallos*, the Greek word for "beautiful," which is then followed by the phrase "and God called" (*ekalesen*). And Christians link this created order both with a radical fall marked by sin and death and with a new creation that overcomes this sin and death, made a present reality in the unification of heaven and earth in the resurrected and glorified body of Christ.

The quintessence, *or what the Greeks called* logos, *was the cosmic principle in which the totality of the universe cohered.*

We can see from the earliest evidence available to us that the Incarnation was understood by Christians in distinctly cosmic terms. In addition to the prologue of John, Paul's first letter to the Corinthians describes God the Father and the Lord Jesus Christ in what biblical scholar Greg Sterling calls prepositional metaphysics, in which the dynamics of the cosmos were described with terms like "from," "in," and "through." Thus Paul said: "For us, there is one God the Father, *from* (*ek*) whom are all things and we *in* (*eis*) him, and one Lord Jesus Christ, *through* (*dia*) whom are all things and we *through* (*dia*) him" (1 Corinthians 8:6, author's translation).[2] Similarly, in Colossians 1:15–20, Christ is depicted as the one through whom all things are created and in whom all things cohere. Indeed, in Christ, all things are made new (Revelation 21:5).

Furthermore, the Hebraic conception of creation upon which Christianity rests provides us with a fundamentally different conception of the human person than that of the Greeks. For Plato, there is a distinction between the spiritual world and the material world,

2. See Gregory E. Sterling, "Prepositional Metaphysics in Jewish Wisdom Speculation and Early Christian Liturgical Texts," *Studia Philonica Annual* 9 (1997): 219–238.

the *eidon* and *eikon*, and the human soul belonged properly to the divine order, the *eidon*, the realm of the forms. The soul, being eternal, was in fact frustrated by its embodiment in the material order. With the advent of Christianity, both the cosmos and the human soul are radically rearranged: the human soul now belongs properly to the created order. It is no more divine than the creation, and thus there is no possibility of an eternally pre-existing soul. In the words of Andrew Louth: "The soul has nothing in common with God; there is no kinship between it and the divine. Its kinship is with its body, in virtue of their common creation, rather than with God."[3]

With the advent of Christianity, both the cosmos and the human soul are radically rearranged: the human soul now belongs properly to the created order.

Instead, the human person is recast as created "in the image of God," which is translated in the Septuagint as *kat' eikona tou Theou*, "according to the image of God." The preposition *kata* has the significance of "in accordance with," and thus most early Greek fathers interpreted this phrase to mean that humans were created in accordance with the Logos, who is "the image of the invisible God" (Colossians 1:15), through whom all things were made. So for the Greek patristics our very creation entails a relationship not merely to God as creator but also to Christ as God Incarnate, the image of the invisible God.[4]

And this is why for the early Greek theologians the Incarnation is so important to the realization of our true humanity. When we were first created in Paradise, we were created to discern and delight in creation as a reflection of the *Logos* through whom all things were

3. Andrew Louth, *The Origins of the Christian Mystical Tradition*, 77.
4. Andrew Louth, "Later Theologians of the Greek East," in Philip F. Esler, ed., *The Early Christian World, Vol. 1* (London: Routledge, 2000), 580-601.

made, and hence we were able to understand ourselves as creatures created in that Image. But in the Fall, this vision is frustrated; it is marred by the tyranny of sin, death, and the devil. And so, the created order, the Paradise that was to serve as the habitat that shaped and sanctified the human person, has now been restored in the Incarnation of the *Logos*, the second person of the Trinity.[5] Indeed, this is the classical significance of the Eucharistic meal, where the grain and fruit of the third day of creation are transformed into the bread and wine identified with the body and blood of Christ, such that creation and Incarnation come together to restore our communion with God and one another.

Gregory of Nyssa, Infinity, and *Epektasis*

This recalibration of the cosmos around Christ the *Logos* had highly determinative implications for distinctly Christian conceptions of Truth, Goodness, and Beauty. Here I want to focus in on two representatives of the Eastern Christian tradition who were highly formative in the development of that tradition, starting with Gregory of Nyssa (ca. AD 335–394).

Gregory of Nyssa is credited with developing New Testament insights into a profoundly aesthetic vision of the relationship between God, creation, and the human person. He developed an unprecedented conception of divine "infinity" (*apeiria*) particularly as it relates to the Good. For Gregory, the goodness of God entails the fact that God has no limits, that He is absolute in His infinity:

> The Good, as long as it is incapable of its opposite, has no bounds to its goodness. . . . Strength is topped

5. See, for example, Athanasius, *On the Incarnation*, transl. Sister Penelope Lawson (Crestwood, NY: St. Vladimir's Seminary Press, 2002).

> only when weakness seizes it; life is limited by death alone; darkness is the ending of light. . . . But if the Divine and unalterable nature is incapable of degeneracy, as even our foes allow, we must regard it as absolutely unlimited in its goodness: and the unlimited is the same as the infinite.[6]

Because God is boundless, without limit, transcending any contrary or opposite, He is an "immense ocean" or sea of Being, beyond comparison, and thus "ineffable and incomprehensible."[7] And Gregory envisioned the infinite emanating or spilling out into the finite in aesthetic splendor through God's act of creation, which manifests materially the glory of God through its participation in His divine Goodness and Beauty.

> Epektasis *involves . . . an intense desire or longing, an ardent love on the part of the human soul to be filled with the inexhaustible plenitude of God's infinite Beauty.*

For Gregory, what is so important here is that the created nature of material reality entails movement and directionality. The very fact that we as creatures have moved from nonbeing to being, from nonexistence to existence, means that the human person is always either drawn toward or away from God. As a creature, there is no such thing as being stagnant. We rise out of the dust moving toward God or away from God. It is in this drawing of the soul either toward or away from God that Gregory developed his distinctive aesthetic theology, for it is the mind's perception of Beauty that serves as the gravitational pull one way or the other. According to Gregory: "there is always something towards which the will is tending, the appetency for moral Beauty naturally drawing it on to movement, this Beauty

---

6. Gregory of Nyssa, "Against Eunomius" I.15, in *Dogmatic Treatises*, trans. William Moore and Henry Austin Wilson, vol. 5, *Nicene and Post-Nicene Fathers* (Peabody, MA: Hendrickson, 2004).
7. Ibid., II.3.

is in one instance really such in its nature, in another it is not so, only blossoming with an illusive appearance of Beauty; and the criterion of these two kinds is the mind that dwells within us."[8]

Now, we saw something very similar to this in Plato. For Plato, true Beauty awakens *eros* or love or desire within the human person, which serves as the gravitational pull that draws us into an encounter with the True and the Good. False Beauty awakens not love but lust, *epithymia,* within us and thus draws us away from the True and the Good. Beauty attracts, whereas lies seduce.

For Gregory, this divine gravitational pull is *epektasis*, which is based on Paul's usage of the verb *epekteinomai* ("extension" or "reaching") in Philippians 3:13.[9] *Epektasis* involves for Gregory an intense desire or longing, an ardent love on the part of the human soul to be filled with the inexhaustible plenitude of God's infinite Beauty. This is what God uses to awaken a love within us and thus draw us up into a relationship with Himself. Gregory described this longing in his work *The Life of Moses*, which reimagines Moses's life as paradigmatic for a distinctly Christian conception of spiritual ascent:

> Such an experience seems to me to belong to the soul which loves what is beautiful. Hope always draws the soul from the Beauty which is seen to what is beyond, always kindles the desire for the hidden through what is constantly perceived. Therefore, the ardent lover of Beauty, although receiving what is always visible as an image of what he desires, yet longs to be filled with the very stamp of the archetype. And the bold request which goes up the mountains of desire asks this: to enjoy the Beauty not in mirrors or reflections, but face to face.[10]

---

8. Gregory of Nyssa, "The Great Catechism" XXI, in *Dogmatic Treatises*, trans. William Moore and Henry Austin Wilson, vol. 5, *Nicene and Post-Nicene Fathers* (Peabody, MA: Hendrickson, 2004).
9. The term "*epektasis*" was given to this motif in Gregory's thought by Jean Daniélou, *Platonisme et théologie mystique* (Paris: Aubier, 1944), 291–307.
10. Gregory of Nyssa, *The Life of Moses*, trans. Abraham J. Malherbe and Everett Ferguson (New York: Paulist Press, 1978), II.231–232.

The key characteristic of this stretching out of the soul toward God is its eternal dynamic: given the Goodness of God in His infinity, there is no end in this longing, for no matter how much one is filled with divine Beauty, one longs for more. The eternal dynamic of *epektasis*, however, should not be confused with a frustrated soul, since the eternal longing for ever more divine glory is itself the fruit of the *satisfaction* that the soul experiences in its encounter with divine Beauty. As John Rist observes: "*Epektasis* is *eros* without frustration as the lover is more and more fully blended with the infinite."[11] Or perhaps we might think of this as what Paul Blowers calls a "sublime frustration, an ongoing process of mystical union with God, with every spiritual advance being merely a new beginning in the never-ending mystery."[12] This "sublime frustration" for Gregory is the love awakened within the soul by God's Beauty. Gregory used both *eros* and *agape* "to describe this love, a love which is essentially a desire for union with the beloved."[13] Salvation is thus a reunification of the soul with the inner life of God, being drawn into the infinite plenitude of Trinitarian life through the physics of love awakened by divine Beauty.

Thus, while Gregory may sound like Plato, there is a radical difference in that Plato's world of the forms cares nothing about us; it does not seek after us and certainly does not die for us. Hence, for Gregory, this *epektasis*, this eternal traversing of God's infinity, involves an eternal communion with the God revealed in Christ, who is the self-replenishing fountain of love and delight, an infinite sea of absolute Beauty.[14]

11. John Rist, "On the Platonism of Gregory of Nyssa," *Hermathena* 169 (Winter 2000): 145.
12. Paul M. Blowers, "Maximus the Confessor, Gregory of Nyssa, and the Concept of 'Perpetual Progress,'" *Vigiliae Christianae* 46, no. 2 (June 1992): 151.
13. Louth, *Origins of the Christian Mystical Tradition*, 96.
14. For a masterful exposition of these themes in Gregory's writings, see David Bentley Hart, *The Beauty of the Infinite: The Aesthetics of Christian Truth* (Grand Rapids: Eerdmans Publishing Company, 2003).

Dionysius the Areopagite and the Divine Names

Gregory's vision of the eternal ascent of the soul into the infinite Goodness and Beauty that is the inner life of God was developed further by a writer from the beginning of the sixth century known to us only under the pseudonym Dionysius the Areopagite. The name originates in the New Testament, where in Acts 17:34 one named Dionysius of the Areopagus is reported to have been converted by Paul by his apologetic for the Christian faith delivered on Mars Hill. For whatever reason, several centuries later, a Christian writer (perhaps a monk) wrote under this name a number of works that became perhaps the most influential writings in Byzantine theology and, as we shall see, made a significant contribution to the development of Latin scholasticism, particularly in the work of Thomas Aquinas.[15]

Dionysius draws together Truth, Goodness, and Beauty in a unique cosmic vision where the whole of the created order is envisioned as continuously praising God through the divinely revealed names of God.

Dionysius drew together Truth, Goodness, and Beauty in a unique cosmic vision where the whole of the created order is envisioned as continuously praising God through the divinely revealed names of God. The revelation of God's names discloses His character and His glory, His attributes that are otherwise beyond the comprehension of finite creatures. It is through the contemplation of the divine names that the human soul is drawn up into a union

15. See Andrew Louth, *Denys the Areopagite* (Wilton, CT: Morehouse-Barlow, 1989), 1–2.

with God through a sequential process of purification, illumination, and perfection or union (*katharsis*, *photismos*, *teleiosis* or *henosis*).[16]

For Dionysius, the first of God's names is the "Good," "which the sacred writers have preeminently set apart for the supra-divine God from all other names."[17] Dionysius followed Plato in positing a priority of the Good over Being, which he illustrated with the Platonic example of the Good being likened to the sun:

> Think of how it is with our sun . . . by the very fact of its existence it gives light to whatever is able to partake of its light, in its own way. So it is with the Good. Existing far above the sun, an archetype far superior to its dull image, it sends the rays of its undivided goodness to everything with the capacity, such as this may be, to receive it. These rays are responsible for all intelligible and intelligent beings, for every power and every activity. . . . They abide in the goodness of God and draw from it the foundation of what they are, their coherence, their vigilance, their home. Their longing for the Good makes them what they are and confers on them their well-being.[18]

As all things participate in the Good, they comprise a hierarchical chain of being, a cosmic order, in which they all interconnect through their mutual relatedness.[19] All things in the created order are good only insofar as they participate in and reflect their proportion and order assigned by the Good. Thus the Areopagite wrote: "The Good returns all things to itself and gathers together whatever may be scattered, for it is the divine Source and unifier of the sum total of all things. Each being looks to it as a source, as

---

16. Louth, *Origins of the Christian Mystical Tradition*, 163.
17. Pseudo-Dionysius, *The Divine Names*, in *The Complete Works*, trans. Colm Luibheid (New York: Paulist Press, 1987), IV.1: 693B. Hereafter I will refer to *The Divine Names* simply as *DN*.
18. *DN* IV.1: 696A.
19. *DN* IV.2: 696B.

the agent of cohesion, and as an objective."[20] Dionysius's universe has thus been likened to "a cascade of beauties springing forth from the First Principle, a dazzling radiance of sensuous splendours which diversify in all created being."[21] It is the divine Good that accounts for the integrity, form, and order inherent in the cosmos.

All things in the created order are good only insofar as they participate in and reflect their proportion and order assigned by the Good.

But what holds this cosmic order in place? How do all things rightly participate in the Good and hence manifest their mutuality and interrelatedness? Dionysius identified the Beautiful as that divine attribute that draws all things into the Good. Following Plato, Dionysius noted the etymological connection between *kallos* (Beauty) and *kalein* (to call): "Beauty 'bids' all things to itself (whence it is called 'Beauty') and gathers everything into itself."[22] Like the Good, Beauty confers beauty on all finite, contingent things in a hierarchical fashion that by its nature directs and draws all things toward their beautifying source. The divine Beauty is therefore

> the beautiful beyond all. It is forever so, unvaryingly, unchangeably so, beautiful but not as something coming to birth and death, to growth or decay, not lovely in one respect while ugly in some other way. It is not beautiful "now" but otherwise "then," beautiful in relation to one thing but not to another. It is not beautiful in one place and not so in another, as though it could be beautiful for some and not for others. Ah no! In itself and by itself it is the uniquely and the eternally beautiful. It is the super-

---

20. *DN* IV.4: 700A.
21. Umberto Eco, *The Aesthetics of Thomas Aquinas* (Cambridge, MA: Harvard University Press, 1988), 23.
22. *DN* IV.7: 701D; see Plato, *Cratylus, Parmenides, Greater Hippias, Lesser Hippias*, ed. and trans. by Harold North Fowler, Loeb Classical Library (Cambridge: Harvard University Press, 1926), 416c.

> abundant source in itself of the Beauty of every beautiful thing. In that simple but transcendent nature of all beautiful things, Beauty and the beautiful uniquely preexisted in terms of their source. From this Beauty comes the existence of everything, each being exhibiting its own way of Beauty. For Beauty is the cause of harmony, of sympathy, of community. Beauty unites all things and is the source of all things. It is the great creating cause which bestirs the world and holds all things in existence by the longing inside them to have Beauty. And there it is ahead of all as Goal, as the Beloved, as the Cause toward which all things move, since it is the longing for Beauty which actually brings them into being.[23]

We may note here the threefold simultaneity between the Beautiful and the Good, for like the Good, the Beautiful is the cause of all things, the goal in the consummation of all things, and the agent through which all things reach their goal. By contemplating all things in the created order as they participate in God's Goodness and Beauty, the human soul is awakened to the inner life of God and thereby realizes its own purpose and goal. Thus Dionysius concluded:

> To put the matter briefly, all being derives from, exists in, and is returned toward the Beautiful and the Good. Whatever there is, whatever comes to be, is there and has being on account of the Beautiful and the Good. All things look at it. All things are moved by it. All things are preserved by it. Every source exists for the sake of it, because of it, and in it and this is so whether such source be exemplary, final, efficient, formal, or elemental. In short, every source, all preservation and ending, everything in fact, derives from the Beautiful and the Good.[24]

Along with his conception of the Beautiful and the Good, Dionysius elucidated a uniquely paradoxical conception of Truth. Dionysius

23. *DN* IV.7: 701D–704A.
24. *DN* IV.10: 705D.

observed that every statement about God postulated by limited, finite creatures such as ourselves entails limitations concomitant with our finiteness and thus falls short of expressing the true nature of God. God is not Himself an object in this world and thus cannot be known; but God has indeed revealed Himself in this world, and the extent of this self-disclosure is the extent of our true knowledge of Him. Dionysius introduced into the Christian lexicon a Neo-Platonic term, "*apophatic* theology," a theology of negation, connoting the idea that what is affirmed by God through His revelation to us (what Dionysius would refer to as "*kataphatic* theology") does not exhaust His own self-disclosure. This means that all our affirmations of God entail a concomitant denial of what we are affirming. God is most certainly love (1 John 4:8) and yet, because of His infinite nature (note the negation of "finite"), His love is in fact incomprehensible and unsearchable (Romans 11:33). Thus, far from negating any attributes of God, apophatic theology *affirms* that God transcends all human categories and language.[25] God is invisible, indescribable, ineffable, infinite, boundless, uncontainable, and incomprehensible. Notice that all these terms are terms of negation; we affirm who God is by saying what He is not. Thus, we may affirm God to be Beautiful as He has disclosed Himself to us through creation and Incarnation, Word and sacrament, but in doing so we must recognize that God's Beauty is itself incomprehensible and ineffable, and thus extends beyond all human description.

For Dionysius, communion with this infinite plenitude of Being is the goal and purpose, indeed the destiny, of all creation. For the divine names of the Good, the Beautiful, and the True extend universally into all things as divine Love, which Dionysius understood to be "a capacity to effect a unity, an alliance, and a particular commingling in the Beautiful and the Good."[26] And it is this Love that serves as a cosmic "yearning," a divine physics that draws together God, the human soul,

25. Louth, *Denys the Areopagite*, 87–88.
26. *DN* IV.12: 709C.

and the whole of creation into a rapturous union with the Good and the Beautiful:

> This divine yearning brings ecstasy so that the lover belongs not to self but to the beloved. . . . This is why the great Paul, swept along by his yearning for God and seized of its ecstatic power, had this inspired word to say: "It is no longer I who live, but Christ who lives in me." Paul was truly a lover and, as, he says, he was beside himself for God, possessing not his own life but the life of the One for whom he yearned, as exceptionally beloved. And in truth, it must be said too that the very cause of the universe in the beautiful, good superabundance of his benign yearning for all is also carried outside of himself in the loving care he has for everything. He is, as it were, beguiled by goodness, by love, and by yearning and is enticed away from his transcendent dwelling place and comes to abide within all things, and he does so by virtue of his supernatural and ecstatic capacity to remain, nevertheless, within himself. . . . In this way he proves himself to be zealous because zeal is always felt for what is desired, and because he is zealous for the creatures for whom he provides. In short, both the yearning and the object of that yearning belong to the Beautiful and the Good. They preexist in it, and because of it they exist and come to be.[27]

The cosmos is thus a glorious manifestation of Divine Love, a beatific union of God and His creation, consummated in an eternal symphony of divine praise. It is this Love that awakens a comparable love within us, which serves to draw us ardently into the inner life of God, and thus restores us back to Paradise.

27. *DN* IV.13: 712A–B.

For Dionysius, communion with this infinite plenitude of Being is the goal and purpose, indeed the destiny, of all creation.

SUMMARY

We have thus far seen that Truth, Goodness, and Beauty in the Christian tradition of the Greek East are rooted in a highly unique conception of God, the cosmos, and the human person. The cosmos is in fact filled with divine meaning and purpose, threatened by the Fall and restored in the Incarnation, which in turn evokes quite purposefully a particular kind of piety within the human person. The human person is created in the image of God in order to respond to the diaphanous cosmos that reveals God's Truth, Goodness, and Beauty. Having been frustrated by the Fall, the cosmos is now redeemed in Christ, who evokes an ardent desire—a love—for God in the human person, who is drawn back into fellowship with God through contemplating the divine attributes of the True, the Good, and the Beautiful in anticipation of the consummation of all things, when heaven and earth are forever one.

CHAPTER FOUR
Truth, Goodness, and Beauty in the Christian World, Part II

The Latin West

INTRODUCTION

Having surveyed key contributions to Truth, Goodness, and Beauty in the Greek East, we now turn to the Latin West and two of its most important exponents: Augustine of Hippo (AD 354–430) and Thomas Aquinas (AD 1225–1274).

AUGUSTINE

In his *Confessions*, Augustine described his pre-Christian life as one characterized by the pursuit of the social ambition and economic success that a Greco-Roman rhetorical education promised. However, this quest was interrupted by his encounter with Cicero's *Hortensius*. During this literary encounter, something awakened within Augustine. He discovered a yearning for a meaning and a purpose outside himself; he found that he longed for a Beauty that could awaken him from his self-centered slumbers, that his heart ached for a life filled with wonder and awe. Augustine found that what makes us human is an insatiable desire to encounter the True, Good, and Beautiful in a life-transforming way, a way that enables our souls to reach for and embrace a state of being of which none greater can possibly be thought, summed up in the opening prayer of his *Confessions*: "… for thou hast made us for thyself and restless is our heart until it comes to rest in thee."[1]

[Augustine] discovered a yearning for a meaning and a purpose outside himself; he found that he longed for a Beauty that could awaken him from his self-centered slumbers, that his heart ached for a life filled with wonder and awe.

It is this extraordinarily personal experience of God, so uniquely characteristic of Augustinian contemplation, that provides the template for the soul's encounter with Truth, Goodness, and Beauty. For it is through entering the inner recesses of the soul as they are informed by the Christian Scriptures that we come to know God as infinitely resplendent in Trinitarian life. And this is because to know oneself truly involves knowing oneself as an image of divine life. By knowing and loving itself precisely as an *image*, the soul is in fact directed toward the God whose image it bears.

The Flash of Truth

This movement from the soul as image of God to the divine source of that image begins with the soul's encounter with Truth. For Augustine, Truth is not simply an abstract principle or postulate; Truth ultimately is a Person. In his later work *On the Trinity*, Augustine described the beginning of the soul's quest for God with this exhortation:

> Come, and see if you can, O *soul weighed down with the body that decays* (Wis 9:15) and burdened with many and

1. Augustine, *Confessions*, transl. Albert C. Outler (Philadelphia: Westminster Press, 1955), I.1.

> variable earthy thoughts, come see it if you can—God is truth. For it is written *that God is light* (1 Jn 1:5) not such as these eyes see, but such as the mind sees when it hears "He is truth." Do not ask what truth is; immediately a fog of bodily images and a cloud of fancies will get in your way and disturb the bright fair weather that bursts on you the first instant when I said "truth." Come, hold it in that first moment in which so to speak you caught a flash from the corner of your eye when the word "truth" was spoken, stay there if you can.[2]

Commenting on this passage, Andrew Louth writes: "The soul, awakened by the flash of vision, longs for the truth, longs to be able to contemplate the truth not just fleetingly, but in an abiding way. So it is a longing that cannot be satisfied with any particular goods, any particular truths, but only with the Good Itself, the Truth Itself—God Himself."[3]

> *The soul, awakened by the flash of vision, longs for the truth, longs to be able to contemplate the truth not just fleetingly, but in an abiding way.*

Indeed, it is by encountering Truth that the soul transforms into a true image of God by complementing its knowledge (*scientia*) with wisdom (*sapientia*). This distinction is essential for Augustine in that knowledge involves the temporal world while wisdom involves eternal reality. It is only through *sapientia* that the soul can be directed toward eternal reality and therefore constitute a true image of God. However, the soul is trapped in *scientia*; humanity, plagued by the imprisonment of the Fall, lacks the spiritual resources constitutive of *sapientia*. This anthropological chasm between *scientia* and *sapientia* is bridged by the Incarnation, the Word made flesh, "*in whom are*

2. Augustine, *On the Trinity*, VIII.3.
3. Andrew Louth, *The Origins of the Christian Mystical Tradition: From Plato to Denys* (Oxford: Oxford University Press, 1981), 149–150.

hidden all the treasures of wisdom and knowledge (Col 2:3)."[4] It is thus through faith in Christ, the incarnate Word who is the Truth, that our souls are graced with *sapientia* and thereby become truly human.

The *Summum Bonum*

Furthermore, Augustine associated the divine and salvific gift of wisdom with his conception of the Good. For Augustine, the *summum bonum*, the supreme good, is God Himself, that Good which exists immutably and eternally, that Good of which none greater can be conceived. However, in light of his doctrine of creation, Augustine saw this Good as constituting a measure or standard in relation to which all finite and temporal constituents derive their goodness. For Augustine, all things are good in relation to their divinely designated position within the hierarchy of God's creation. Things are not evil in and of themselves but become evil when their order is abused. For example, a ham sandwich is good in itself, but if someone prioritizes the ham sandwich above, say, a child, then God's hierarchy of goods has been violated. All things are to be valued and loved in accordance with their proportionate value in the divine economy. Augustine developed this perspective of ordered loves (*ordo amoris*) in his *On Christian Doctrine*. In book I, chapters 3 and 4, he makes a distinction between things that are enjoyed and things that are used. We enjoy things when we love them for their own sakes; we use things when we love them for the sake of something else. For Augustine, only God is worthy of being loved for His own sake, for He alone is supremely valuable. All other loves are subordinate to the love of God; all created things are to be loved as objects that cause us to delight in God.

*It is by encountering Truth that the soul transforms into a true image of God by complementing its knowledge (*scientia*) with wisdom (*sapientia*).*

4. Augustine, *On the Trinity* XIII.24.

And it is here, in this *ordo amoris*, that we discover the significance of wisdom (*sapienta*) for Augustine's account of the Good, for it is in acquiring wisdom that the human soul realizes its divinely designated place in God's cosmic economy. Augustine saw humanity's attempt to know God on its own terms as prideful, which is the heart of the Fall. Thus, it is the humility of the Son in His Incarnation that ameliorates the pride of man. By awakening us to the wisdom of God, Christ enables the human person to once again take his or her place in the divine economy and hence rightly order his or her loves, as all things are appropriated as occasions for delighting in God.

Beauty and Divine Life

Furthermore, the notions of *sapientia* and *ordo amoris* provide the basic frames of reference for Augustine's quest for Beauty. As early as his *Confessions*, Augustine imagined Beauty in terms of the harmony of the cosmic order of things, an aesthetic order that serves, in Platonic fashion, as a ladder of ascent to divine life:

> I asked myself why I approved of the Beauty of bodies, whether celestial or terrestrial, and what justification I had for giving an unqualified judgment on mutable things, saying "This ought to be thus, and that ought not to be thus." In the course of this inquiry why I made such value judgments as I was making, I found the unchangeable and authentic eternity of truth to transcend my mutable mind. And so step by step I ascended from bodies to the soul which perceives through the body, and from there to its inward force. . . . From there again I ascended to the power of reasoning to which is to be attributed the power of judging the deliverances of the bodily senses. This power . . . withdrew itself from the contradictory swarms of imaginative fantasies, so as to discover the light by which it was flooded. At that point it had no hesitation in declaring that the unchangeable is

preferable to the changeable, and that on this ground it can know the unchangeable, since, unless it could somehow know this, there would be no certainty in preferring it to the mutable. So in the flash of a trembling glance it attained to that which is.[5]

Thus, as with Plato and the Greek Fathers, Beauty serves the indispensable role of momentum toward God, a gravitational pull that draws the soul onward toward the True and the Good.

As with the quest for Truth, the mind is central to this aesthetic ascent. As we have already observed, the human soul is incapable of contemplating divine reality, being trapped within itself because of the Fall. Divine grace is necessary to transform the mind into a sapient instrument through which the soul can know and love God. This anthropological deprivation is highly pertinent to Augustine's conception of Beauty. In one of his earliest writings, *Answer to Skeptics*, Augustine observed an etymological relationship between reflected Beauty, or "philocaly," and "philosophy," the love of wisdom:

> hence, the splendor and the most orderly arrangement of all things—and the charm of a reflected Beauty everywhere, adorning everything. This is commonly called philocaly . . . philocaly and philosophy have very similar surnames. They would seem to be—truly, they are—of the same family, so to speak. In fact, what is philosophy? It is love of wisdom. And what is philocaly? It is love of Beauty. Consult the Greeks on this point. But, what is wisdom? Is it not the true Beauty itself? Therefore, those two are assuredly akin, begotten of the same parent.[6]

We may note here that love (*philos*) is what Beauty and wisdom share in common. The love that is awakened within the human person

5. Augustine, *Confessions*, trans. Henry Chadwick (Oxford: Oxford University Press, 1992), VII.17.
6. Augustine, *The Happy Life, Answer to Skeptics, Divine Providence and the Problem of Evil, Soliloquies*, trans. Ludwig Schopp (Washington, DC: Catholic University of America Press, 1948), II:2–3.

through philosophy and given by the Holy Spirit is nothing less than a love for Beauty that draws the soul toward God. As Carol Harrison observes: "This love [Augustine] describes as a dynamic principle in man—it cannot be still, but must draw him, as a weight, irresistibly towards its object."[7] Thus, in one of his more notable poetic moments, Augustine wrote:

> Late have I loved you, Beauty so old and so new: late have I loved you. And see, you were within and I was in the external world and sought you there, and in my unlovely state I plunged into those lovely created things which you made. You were with me, and I was not with you. The lovely things kept me far from you, though if they did not have their existence in you, they had no existence at all. You called and cried out loud and shattered my deafness. You were radiant and resplendent, you put to flight my blindness. You were fragrant, and I drew in my breath and now pant after you. I tasted you, and I feel but hunger and thirst for you. You touched me, and I am set on fire to attain the peace which is yours.[8]

Thus, as with Plato and the Greek Fathers, Beauty serves the indispensible role of momentum toward God, a gravitational pull that draws the soul onward toward the True and the Good.

Beauty thus draws the believing soul into an encounter with God. Hence Harrison notes that the love that the Holy Spirit awakens within the human person for Beauty is always inseparable from the Good and the True, for it is ultimately a love that draws one into

7. Carol Harrison, *Beauty and Revelation in the Thought of Saint Augustine* (Oxford: Clarendon Press, 1992), 254.
8. Augustine, *Confessions*, trans. by Henry Chadwick, X.27.

union with God.[9] For Augustine, like the Greek fathers, the quest for Truth, Goodness, and Beauty is none other than a quest for God Himself, an ascent of the soul into the inner recesses of divine life. The end of such a quest is nothing less than an encounter with the Beatific Vision, the ineffable eternal beholding of the infinite Beauty of God:

> How great shall be that felicity, which shall be tainted with no evil, which shall lack no good, and which shall afford leisure for the praises of God, who shall be all in all . . . and, along with the other great and marvelous discoveries which shall then kindle rational minds in praise of the great Artificer, there shall be the enjoyment of a Beauty which appeals to the reason. . . . God Himself, who is the Author of virtue, shall there be its reward; for, as there is nothing greater or better, He has promised Himself. . . . He shall be the end of our desires who shall be seen without end, loved without cloy, praised without weariness. . . . There we shall rest and see, see and love, love and praise. This is what shall be in the end without end.[10]

Thomas Aquinas

By the time of Thomas Aquinas in the thirteenth century, cosmic values in the West had developed into what has been termed the "doctrine of transcendentals." As represented in the work of thirteenth-century scholars such as Philip the Chancellor, Alexander of Hales, and Albert the Great (who was Aquinas's teacher), the doctrine of transcendentals involved identifying those properties of perfection in which all things participate in some degree as a necessary condition for

9. Harrison, *Beauty and Revelation*, 256.

10. Augustine, *City of God*, in Philip Schaff, ed., *City of God, Christian Doctrine*, vol. 2, *Nicene and Post-Nicene Fathers* (Peabody, MA: Hendrickson, 2004), XXII.30.

their existence.[11] For example, if we have before us a flower, a tree, and a cat, we may observe that all three share something in common: they all *exist.* And yet, while the flower, the tree, and the cat all exist, they do not exhaust that existence; in fact, the only way that they all share in or participate in existence is if existence extends beyond any one of these particulars. Indeed, all particular things that constitute the entire universe are currently participating in an existence that is wholly other than the sum total of all existing things.

The doctrine of transcendentals established four common and primary notions in which all things participate: Being, Unity or One, the True, and the Good. It was believed that these four notions were convertible with one another in that they were interchangeable; whatever is predicated for or identified with one is the case for the others; they entail one another, such that wherever you have one you have the other three. Thus Being, Unity, the True, and the Good constituted together a synthetic vision of divine life in which all things rest and have their existence.[12]

The doctrine of transcendentals established four common and primary notions in which all things participate: Being, Unity or One, the True, and the Good.

Being, Truth, and Goodness

For Aquinas, the most important of the transcendentals is Being. Aquinas recognized that to say "something *is*," e.g., something is True or Good, is to ascribe that something with Being. Aquinas saw Being as basic to all other transcendentals, in that Unity, the True, and the Good all have Being.

11. Jan A. Aertsen, *Medieval Philosophy and the Transcendentals: The Case of Thomas Aquinas* (Leiden: Brill, 1996), 31.
12. Ibid.

Furthermore, if all things (e.g., the flower, the tree, and the cat) participate in Being then Being by definition must be a Unity; it must be single. Otherwise, all things would be participating in different beings, not in Being itself. If all things share in Being, then there must be a single or unified Being in which all things share.

In determining the nature of the True and the Good, Aquinas drew from a micro-macro schema with which we are now familiar. The human soul is differentiated into intellect and will, which are the microcosmic faculties that correspond to macrocosmic Being. The intellect relates to Being in terms of Truth, in that Truth expresses Being in the form of knowledge; the will relates to Being in terms of the Good, in that Goodness expresses Being in the form of the appetite or affections. As Jan Aertsen notes: "The triad 'being-true-good' corresponds, as formal objects, with the triad 'soul-intellect-will.'"[13]

And so Aquinas provides us with this macro-micro triad:

Being—soul

True—intellect

Good—will

Beauty and the Transcendentals

However, the topic of Beauty (*pulchritudo, species, formositas*) and the Beautiful (*pulchrum*) in Aquinas remains controversial for scholars, who have been perplexed, given the historical precedent in both the Greek East and the Latin West, over the omission of Beauty among the transcendentals in Aquinas's work. In this regard, Aquinas seems to be following Aristotle, who also omits Beauty among the transcendental properties of Unity, Goodness, and Truth.[14] Aertsen has argued that Beauty for Aquinas does not express a mode of Being

13. Ibid., 260.
14. Cf. Aristotle, *Metaphysics*, ed. and trans. by Hugh Tredennick, 2 vols., Loeb Classical Library (Cambridge: Harvard University Press, 1933-35), 6, 8; Aristotle, *The Nichomachean Ethics*, ed. and trans. by H. Rackham, Loeb Classical Library (Cambridge: Harvard University Press), 1968. 1.

peculiar to itself and therefore cannot be considered a transcendental.[15] Instead, Aertsen considers Beauty simply an extension of the Good in Aquinas's thought. For example, in Aquinas's *Summa Theologica*, he defined the Beautiful in the context of his larger discussion on the Good.[16] And later, the threefold attributes Aquinas ascribed to Beauty—proportion, integrity, and clarity—are in the context of his extended discussion on the Beauty of the second Person of the Trinity, the Son, whom Aquinas saw as Beauty par excellence.[17]

"There is a twofold harmony on things. The first is according to the relations of creatures to God. . . . The second kind of harmony is present in things by virtue of their ordering among themselves."

However, it is in chapter 4 of his commentary on Dionysius's *Divine Names* that we have Aquinas's most extended discussion on Beauty. Here Aquinas posited a twofold proportionality and harmony that belongs to Beauty:

> There is a twofold harmony on things. The first is according to the relations of creatures to God. [Dionysius] touches on this when he says that God is the cause of harmony, "as calling all things to himself," in that he turns all toward himself as to an end. . . . For this reason Beauty is named *kallos* in Greek, which is derived from the verb "to call." The second kind of harmony is present in things by virtue of their ordering among themselves. [Dionysius] touches this point when he adds that God gathers all things to the same in all. And this can be understood according to the Platonic

15. Aertsen, *Medieval Philosophy*, 337.
16. Thomas Aquinas, *Summa Theologica,* trans. Fathers of the English Dominican Province (NY: Benziger Bros., 1947), I.5.4 ad 1. Hereafter I will refer to *Summa Theologica* simply as *ST*.
17. *ST* I.39.8.

> view that the higher things are present to the lower by participation, while the lower things are in the higher by eminence, and thus all things are in all. Finally, from the fact that all things are in all by some order it follows that all things are ordered to the same ultimate thing.[18]

Here Aquinas keys us into the role of Beauty in the cosmos, with Dionysius acting as the composer. The interconnectedness of all things manifests the proportionality of the cosmos and thus constitutes its Beauty, in that Beauty is proportionality for Aquinas. Like a grand cosmic tapestry, all particulars are weaved together in a harmonious pattern of proportionality.

Beauty for Aquinas thus involves both the complex of the cosmos and the calling to consummation, to divine communion, in which all things are eternally perfected in God.

But we may note as well from this passage that Beauty does not simply endow this cosmic chain of Being with proportionality and continuity but also provides the allure, the momentum, for drawing the cosmos back up into inner Trinitarian life. Beauty, in this second sense, is a movement, a cosmic disposition or orientation toward God as the goal and purpose, the perfector of all things. Beauty for Aquinas thus involves both the complex of the cosmos and the calling to consummation, to divine communion, in which all things are eternally perfected in God.

Now, for Aquinas, it is precisely in this movement of the cosmos back to God that humanity plays such an important role, for humans above all other creatures are endowed with the *imago Dei*, the image of God. Indeed, Aquinas saw the whole of creation as in effect the image of God as it exemplifies God's love for his own Beauty:

---

18. Alice M. Ramos, *Dynamic Transcendentals: Truth, Goodness, and Beauty from a Thomastic Perspective* (Washington, DC: Catholic University of America Press, 2012), 73–74n13.

> It pertains to a perfect agent to act by virtue of love for what it possesses, and for this reason [Dionysius] adds that the beautiful that is God is the efficient, moving, and containing cause, "by a love of his own Beauty." Since he has his own Beauty, he wishes to multiply it as far as possible, that is to say, by means of his likeness.[19]

However, God's love for His own Beauty climaxes *in and through those creatures created most properly in the image of God, creatures of intelligence and volition, Truth and Goodness.* And this is where Dionysius's chain of being kicks in: the proportionality of the cosmos means that all things as an image of God relate to God through those creatures that most properly bear God's image, in the highest sense of the term. It is thus through those creatures endowed microcosmically with Truth and Goodness that all creation participates in God and thereby exemplifies the radiance of divine Beauty. The perfection of the human person through the beautifying extensions of the Incarnation—Word and sacrament—is thus a *cosmic* perfection, wherein all things are returned back to God through Christ, who is Beauty *par excellence.*[20]

In short, the Christian vision of Truth, Goodness, and Beauty is an invitation, a divine call, to awaken the fullness of our humanity as the entire cosmos is incorporated into the transformative life, death, and resurrection of Christ.

19. Ibid., 84.
20. Cf. *ST* I.39.8.

SUMMARY

Both Augustine and Aquinas are situated securely within a pattern of thought evident among the most prominent theorists in the Greek East: Truth, Goodness, and Beauty are divine attributes by which the whole of creation is endowed with meaning and purpose, and focused particularly in microcosmic form in the distinctly human manifestation of the image of God. In the face of the interruption of this divine meaning and purpose through the adverse effects of humanity's fall, the Incarnation restores the human person to his original divine dignity through regeneration in Word and sacrament, thereby restoring the cosmos and reawakening its entailed synthetic vision of the divine attributes of Truth, Goodness, and Beauty. Thus, as Alister McGrath observes, the "Christian tradition insists that all that is true, beautiful, and good finds its fulfillment in Jesus Christ."[21] By encountering Truth, the human intellect is awakened to the infinite wisdom of God revealed in Christ; by encountering Goodness, the human volition is directed to act in accordance with the divine purposefulness of creation and our own created nature renewed in Christ; and by encountering Beauty, the human soul is awakened to the inexhaustible wellspring of divine love revealed in Christ. In short, the Christian vision of Truth, Goodness, and Beauty is an invitation, a divine call, to awaken the fullness of our humanity as the entire cosmos is incorporated into the transformative life, death, and resurrection of Christ. "I have come that they may have life, and have it to the full" (John 10:10).

---

21. Alister E. McGrath, *The Open Secret,* 308.

Chapter Five
Redeeming the Senses: The Aesthetics of Classical Education

Introduction

Our exploration of Truth, Goodness, and Beauty has thus far focused on divine, cosmic, and human frames of reference that began with the pre-Socratics, were developed in the philosophy of Plato, and were radically reappropriated in the formative period of the Christian tradition. Common to all these traditions is the idea that Truth, Goodness, and Beauty are cosmic values that awaken within us our true humanity, drawing us into a harmonious relationship with the cosmos and our fellow man, thereby fulfilling what may be called a cosmic communion or *koinonia* that maintains and perpetuates the life of the world. In the distinctively Christian outworking of these frames of reference, the cosmic radiance of the divine attributes of Truth, Goodness, and Beauty have been frustrated due to Adam's fall, and in turn have been restored in the Incarnation and the redemption of the human person into a renewed Paradise, the "new creation."

Now, there is a further dimension to these cosmic constituents to which we have of yet only alluded. In chapter 2, we discovered that for Plato, the *paideia*—the educational project that sought to teach the soul to detach itself from false things and attach to true things—involved a twofold purification: moral purification and intellectual purification. This twofold purification is represented analogously in the Christian tradition by what we will call the "redemption of the senses" on the one hand and the cultivation of the "moral imagination" on the other. In this chapter, we shall explore the former, particularly in terms of the role of the body in Christian education, which involves a redirecting of the senses away from the carnal and the sensual and toward the eternally True, Good, and Beautiful and thus prepares the body for its resurrection. In order to understood more deeply the nature of educational aesthetics, I want to begin our discussion with an overview of recent research on the importance of the body for human knowledge, and from there demonstrate that this recent emphasis on embodied knowledge has much in common with the classical conception of bodily perception. From there I shall trace out how these somatic frames of reference were developed uniquely in the Christian conception of aesthetic knowledge that involved a comprehensive redemption of the senses. I will then conclude with a few thoughts on how a robust appreciation of the physiognomic nature of knowledge in the Christian tradition provides us with a foundation from which the fine arts can flourish in our current renaissance of classical education.

A Return to Embodiment

In his 1641 *Meditations on First Philosophy,* René Descartes wrote the following:

> Simply by knowing that I exist and seeing at the same time that absolutely nothing else belongs to my nature or essence except that I am a thinking thing, I can infer correctly that my essence consists solely in the fact that I am a thinking thing. It is true that I may have . . . a body that is very closely joined to me. But nevertheless, on the one hand I have a clear and distinct idea of myself, in so far as I am simply a thinking, non-extended thing; and on the other hand I have a distinct idea of body, in so far

> as this is simply an extended, non-thinking thing. And accordingly, it is certain that I am really distinct from my body, and can exist without it.[1]

The Frenchman Descartes laid the foundation for the German tradition of Gottfried Leibniz and Christian Wolff, who both maintained that the senses represented a lower, imperfect, cognitive power in relation to the higher power of the intellect. Immanuel Kant, while following Alexander Baumgarten in rejecting this designation of the senses to a lower form of knowledge, nevertheless famously argued for a "pure reason" that entails formal structures in no way based on anything physical and thus independent of our embodied, phenomenal selves. Kant further argued that moral laws were truly moral only to the extent that they issued from "pure practical reason," detached from feeling, emotion, or bodily constraints.[2]

The recognition of the centrality of the body in human social identity has provided the foundry for a rich appreciation of the role of the body in the shaping of human culture.

However, since the 1950s, this dialectical conception of knowledge has begun to crack under an increasing awareness within the academy of the manifoldness of knowledge. In as much as the mind exists *in* a body, it has been recognized by philosophers, anthropologists, and sociologists alike that we as humans cannot but experience ourselves simultaneously *in* and *as* our bodies.[3] Statements such as "My foot hurts" and "I am in pain" are in fact synonymous state-

1. René Descartes, "Meditations on First Philosophy," in Andrew Bailey, ed., *First Philosophy: Fundamental Problems and Readings in Philosophy*, vol. 2, *Knowledge and Reality* (Toronto: Broadview, 2004), 53.
2. Mark Johnson, *The Meaning of the Body: Aesthetics of Human Understanding* (Chicago: University of Chicago Press, 2012), 7.
3. M. L. Lyon and J. M. Barbalet, "Society's Body: Emotion and the 'Somatization' of Social Theory," in Thomas J. Csordas, ed., *Embodiment and Experience: The Existential Ground of Culture and Self* (Cambridge: Cambridge University Press, 1996), 48–67, 54.

ments that indicate I don't just have a body but I am my body. We experience things done to our bodies as done to ourselves.[4]

The recognition of the centrality of the body in human social identity has provided the foundry for a rich appreciation of the role of the body in the shaping of human culture. In the highly influential *Purity and Danger*, social anthropologist Mary Douglas makes the connection between the physical body and social body, noting that cultural concerns about the body, such as taboo codes, ethical identity, and conceptions of purity, are frequently metaphors for social relationships and boundaries.[5] From this cross-cultural perspective, we should not therefore be surprised to find that St. Paul's conception of the human body as a social organism in 1 Corinthians 12 was in fact a popular rhetorical *topos* in the Greco-Roman world, which idealized social harmony in somatic terms. Furthermore, the relationship between the human body and society has notably been the subject of the research by Pierre Bourdieu, whose theory of *habitus* argues that the body provides a canvas whereby the senses can in fact be shaped by cultural sensibilities.[6] These socially shaped senses include not only the senses proper (taste, touch, smell, etc.) but also a sense of Beauty, a sense of responsibility, a sense of right and wrong, and a sense of humor, hence demonstrating a cultural link between *sense* and the *senses.*[7]

The unconscious way in which we sense the world around us may excuse our Enlightenment sensibilities at least to an extent. Mark Johnson has noted that the bodies that govern best govern least: "We don't have to work to ignore the working of our bod-

4. Meredith B. McGuire, "Religion and the Body: Rematerializing the Human Body in the Social Sciences of Religion," *Journal for the Scientific Study of Religion* 29, no. 3 (1990): 283–296, 284.
5. *Purity and Danger: An Analysis of the Concepts of Pollution and Taboo* (New York: Routledge, 2002).
6. Pierre Bourdieu, *Outline of a Theory of Practice*, trans. Richard Nice (Cambridge: Cambridge University Press, 1977), 124.
7. McGuire, "Religion and the Body," 290; cf. David Howes, "Foreword," in Howes, ed., *The Varieties of Sensory Experience: A Sourcebook in the Anthropology of the Senses* (Toronto: University of Toronto Press, 1991), x.

ies. On the contrary, our bodies hide themselves from us in their very acts of making meaning and experience possible. The way we experience things appears to have a dualistic character."[8] Drew Leder concurs: "Insofar as I perceive through an organ, it necessarily recedes from the perceptual field it discloses. I do not smell my nasal tissue, hear my ear, or taste my taste buds but perceive with and through such organs."[9] This tacit experience of our bodies and its relationship to knowledge has been developed most especially by Michael Polanyi, who argues that these learned tastes and distastes and the cultural shaping of the senses provide what he calls the *subsidiary* means by which we know our world.[10] Polanyi distinguishes between "subsidiary" awareness and "focal" awareness. For example, when someone points something out with his finger, we see the finger, but we are not looking *at* it but rather *through* it, as it were. Our awareness of the finger is the subsidiary means, the instrumentality, by which we may focus on the object to which it points. For Polanyi, all knowledge obtains through a tacit collection of subsidiaries that constitute a framework through which our perception of the world is shaped and focused, very much the way all sight obtains through the instrumentality of the eyes. It is through this tacit awareness that we know our world, a knowledge that is rooted in the body and sensory experience.

It is through this tacit awareness that we know our world, a knowledge that is rooted in the body and sensory experience.

These studies, in short, recognize the inescapably aesthetic nature of knowledge, recovering the centrality of the body in our coming to a knowledge of ourselves and our world. I say *re*covery, since this

8. Johnson, *Meaning of the Body*, 4.
9. Drew Leder, *The Absent Body* (Chicago: University of Chicago Press, 1990), 14–15.
10. Michael Polanyi, *The Tacit Dimension* (New York: Doubleday, 1966).

somatic epistemology is in fact comparable to that found in the classical Greek conception of aesthetic knowledge and its Christian appropriation and development, to which I now turn.

The Redemption of Creation and the Body

Like so much we have seen thus far, the redemption of the senses has its origins in Plato. In *Timaeus*, Plato proposed that the contemplation of the cosmos could lead the soul to God and hence transcend the cosmos. And this contemplation of the cosmos entails an interest in the senses, where sight is appropriated as the foundation of philosophy and the sense that leads to a discovery of divine Truth.[11] In his pursuit of Beauty in the *Symposium*, Plato appropriated *visual* Beauty as what initially inspires the philosopher to mount the "heavenly ladder" to God, who is absolute Beauty.[12] Hearing and the sonic dimension, as well, play an important role in this divine ascent. Plato's pursuit of the Good in his *Republic* outlined his *mysike paideia*, how music and poetry provide the chief means by which rhythm and harmony can be communicated through the body and sunk deeply into the recesses of the soul.[13] This means, for Plato, that both soul and body are deeply sensitive to Beauty, and it is the practice of *theoria*, or contemplation, that unites Beauty, morality, and intellection in the formation of our humanity. Thus the soul ascends into what Plato called "the wide ocean of intellectual Beauty."[14] It is there that we find life, what is eternal and perfect and incorruptible, absolute in its proportion and symmetry, in short, absolute Beauty.

---

11. Anthony Synnott, "Puzzling over the Senses From Plato to Marx," in Howes, *Variety of Sensory Experience*, 61–76, 63.
12. Plato, *Symposium* 210d–211b.
13. Louth, *The Origins of the Christian Mystical Tradition*, 8.
14. Plato, *Symposium* 210a–d.

Following the exhortations of St. Paul and the author of Hebrews in developing a distinctly Christian *paideia* (Ephesians 6:4; 2 Timothy 3:14–17; Hebrews 12:5), Christian writers followed this cosmic trajectory by reflecting on the nature of the cosmos as creation and God as Creator. Second-century hymns such as the *Odes of Solomon* and writers such as Clement and Tertullian celebrated creation as a means by which one can contemplate the very nature of God Himself. In his work *On the Six Days of Creation (Hexaemeron)*, which became paradigmatic for Byzantine creation theology, Basil of Caesarea (AD 330–379) argued that through the revelation of creation one can encounter something of the divine nature:

> Let us glorify the Master Craftsman for all that has been done wisely and skillfully; and from the Beauty of the visible things let us form an idea of Him who is more than beautiful; and from the greatness of [what is perceptible and circumscribed] let us conceive of Him who is infinite and immense and who surpasses all understanding in the plenitude of His power.[15]

For the patristic tradition, this encounter with the divine nature through nature is possible because the divine *Logos* and the created order have in fact joined together in the Incarnation, such that the fourth-century Christian writer Ephrem the Syrian (AD 306–373) could speak of the Old Testament, the New Testament, and nature "as three harps on which the Church played the music of Christ, all proclaiming the same God in perfect harmony."[16]

For Plato, both soul and body are deeply sensitive to Beauty, and it is the practice of theoria, or contemplation, that unites Beauty, morality, and intellection in the formation of our humanity.

15. Quoted in Susan Ashbrook Harvey, *Scenting Salvation: Ancient Christianity and the Olfactory Imagination* (Berkeley: University of California Press, 2006), 59.
16. Quoted in ibid., 60.

However, while the Incarnation has reawakened God's divine glory in creation, such a reawakening remains obscured by the fallen sense humanity has of the world. In this early Christian tradition, the senses have fallen along with the soul and are thus in need of redemption. So the union of heaven and earth in the Incarnation must extend into the sacramental life of the Church in order to awaken the senses to the renewed condition of the created order. Hence, for Ephrem, baptism bestows upon the believer a new physical sense able to receive knowledge of God through sanctified sensory experiences.[17] As we saw above, Augustine, in his *Confessions*, described his experience of encountering the Beauty of God in terms of the divine reconstitution of the senses:

> You [O Lord] called and cried aloud and shattered my deafness. You were radiant and resplendent, you put to flight my blindness. You were fragrant and I drew in my breath and now pant after you. I tasted you, and I feel but hunger and thirst for you. You touched me, and I am set on fire to attain the peace which is yours.[18]

As such, the body, washed in baptism, became the location for Christianity, one that focused on the redemption of the senses in the theater of a distinctly Christian *paideia*. This *paideia* shaped aesthetic sensibilities in accordance with the new creation in Christ.

There are three aesthetic areas in particular within this emerging Christian *paideia* that I will now foreground: sacred sound, sacred sight, and sacred drama.

---

17. Ephrem the Syrian, *Hymns on Faith*, 81.9, cited in Susan Ashbrook Harvey, *Scenting Salvation*, 61, 260 n.21.
18. Augustine, *Confessions*, trans. Henry Chadwick (Oxford: Oxford University Press, 1992), 10.27.38.

Sacred Sound

Given that Christians are referred to as the "called ones" (*kletoi*, 1 Corinthians 1:2), who come to faith through "hearing the word of Christ" (Romans 10:17), the acoustic or sonic dimension of human experience was profoundly shaped by Christianity. The patristic emphasis on the power of words arose largely from the Greco-Roman tradition, which stressed the art of rhetoric for an educated humanity. Both Plato and Aristotle recognized that the soul was deeply affected by the aural reception of rhetorical delivery. Hence Aristotle reflected on the loudness, pitch, and rhythm of the voice for an effective *hypokrisis* or delivery, one that puts the audience into an emotional frame of mind favorable to the orator's case.[19]

It was within this sonic world of rhetoric that a distinctly Christian soundscape emerged, at the center of which was the proclamation of the gospel.

It was within this sonic world of rhetoric that a distinctly Christian soundscape emerged, at the center of which was the proclamation of the gospel. This soundscape, empowered by the Holy Spirit, set the stage for what Carol Harrison has called "transformative listening."[20] Christian rhetoric, embodied in the sermon or homily, sought to awaken the imagination through sound, inspiring the listener not merely to hear but also to understand, to apprehend Scripture as it was interpreted in light of the Christ event. As such, the recitation of Scripture provided a map of the cosmos, recreated in Christ, that served as an aural foundation for reconstituting one's

19. Aristotle, *On Rhetoric*, ed. and trans. by J. H. Freese, Loeb Classical Library (Cambridge: Harvard University Press, 1926), 1403b27–31, 1356a3, 14–16.
20. Carol Harrison, *The Art of Listening in the Early Church* (Oxford: Oxford University Press, 2013).

life as a mimetic imitation of the virtues embedded in this sacred discourse. In the midst of a relatively illiterate populace, Christianized rhetoric had the power to reshape the sonic appetites and expectations of the general population.

It is within this aural context that a distinct sacred music tradition arose within the church. Following the Pythagorean concept of the "music of the spheres" in which the entire cosmos is subject to the same laws of proportion that rule music, sacred music in the church sought to awaken on earth the music of the heavens in order to transform both its music makers and perceivers into heavenly beings. Hence, Gregory Nazianzus (AD 330–390) talked of the role of singing in Christian worship to unite the Christian community on earth with the angels of heaven and thus exemplify the harmony of creation.[21] Maximus the Confessor (AD 580–662) wrote: "In this light, the soul, now equal in dignity with the holy angels . . . and having learned to praise in concert with them . . . is brought to the adoption of similar likeness by grace."[22] Gregory of Nyssa, in a Christmas sermon, conceived of creation as "the temple of the Lord of creation" that was sung into being, and it was this divine song that was to be echoed in the hymns of praise among God's people but was silenced by sin.[23] As a result of the work of Christ, however, people excluded by sin could now rejoin the liturgy of heaven and earth, and in so doing enter into the holy of holies to worship with the angels.

Sacred music in the church sought to awaken on earth the music of the heavens in order to transform both its music makers and perceivers into heavenly beings.

21. Gregory Nazianzus, *Carmina* 2.1.1.180, cited in Margaret Barker, *Temple Themes in Christian Worship* (London: T&T Clark International, 2007), 222.
22. Maximus the Confessor, *Mystagogy* 23, quoted in Barker, *Temple Themes in Christian Worship*, 222.
23. Barker, *Temple Themes*, 225.

Sacred Sight

Along with the acoustic environment, the classical tradition was concerned with the sanctification of the visual as well. For Aristotle, art or *techne* is defined as the "trained ability of making something under the guidance of rational thought."[24] It was the fourth-century painter Pamphilus who introduced panel painting as a school subject and who foreshadowed the rise of the classical *quadrivium* by his insistence on a knowledge of arithmetic and geometry among his art students. Paintings ranged from small-scale works of art for domestic, decorative purposes to heroic portraits of civic leaders and famous battles climaxing into cultic images. Rome used art as a visual display of power: Captured sculptures and paintings from its military conquests were used to adorn triumphal processions, and sculpture was employed as part of rituals of power in the Augustan age.

In early Christianity, artistic symbolism took on significance at least in part due to the multiethnic nature of the growing church, in that this multiethnicity encouraged the use of easily recognized symbols that transcended language barriers.[25] An emerging iconography in the East sought to sanctify the visual, shaping the optical sense with earthly materials transformed into heavenly visions of new creation.[26] Crossing over into the medieval West, the development of Augustinian theology ascribed primacy to the sense of sight in relation to the doctrine of divine illumination. Most notably developed by Bonaventure in his *Reduction of the Arts to Theology*, light became the key motif for understanding, so that just as the physical sight was dependent on physical light, so spiritual sight was dependent on a divine luminosity. Hence for Bonaventure, the illu-

24. Aristotle, *Nichomachean Ethics*, Loeb Classical Library (Cambridge, MA: Harvard University Press, 1994), 1140a9–10.
25. Patrick Reyntiens, "Art, Visual," in Adrian Hastings et al, eds., *The Oxford Companion to Christian Thought* (New York: Oxford University Press, 2000), 41.
26. On the Byzantine iconic tradition, see, for example, Andreas Andreopoulos, *Metamorphosis: The Transfiguration in Byzantine Theology and Iconography* (Crestwood, NY: St. Vladimir's Seminary Press, 2005).

mination of the Holy Spirit on the mind enables us to imaginatively reinterpret the natural world around us as a theater of divine glory, a reinterpretation made explicit in the idealized work of the artisan. Divine illumination entails the overlapping of the natural world with a sanctified imagination, thus transforming the world around us into visions of new creation.

Moreover, Keith Lilley's study on medieval urban planning has highlighted the myriad ways in which the city functioned as a "map" of Christian belief and meaning.[27] For example, the walls that encircled the medieval city represented the cosmos, while the four gates to the city represented the four Gospels as the form of a cross. The orthogonal or straight layout of the city streets not only themselves created crosses, but also were said to represent the call of Isaiah 40:3 and 40:4: "make straight in the desert a highway for our God" and "make crooked places straight."[28] The architectural design of the cathedral at the center of the city sought to explicitly transform the world into a vision of new creation and provided the center for the various festivals and public processions that affirmed Christianity as the foundation of the life of the city.

Divine illumination entails the overlapping of the natural world with a sanctified imagination, thus transforming the world around us into visions of new creation.

Sacred Drama

And finally, both the acoustic and visual senses coalesced into the world of drama and theater. Greek audiences were drawn toward two

---

27. Keith D. Lilley, "Cities of God? Medieval Urban Forms and Their Christian Symbolism," *Transactions of the Institute of British Geographers* New Series 29, no. 3 (September 2004): 296–313.
28. Ibid.

central features in dramatic performances: the dancelike movement of the actors and the sound of the spoken word. The plays were all composed in a variety of meters, and the Greeks listened with open ears not just to the message of the words but to the sound and rhythm of each line.

Aristotle recognized in his *Poetics* that dramatic performances did not so much reflect living as *essentialize* it; that is, dramatic performances present paradigms of life. Artistic imitation thus idealizes the world, representing what is there in our ecology and social and cultural experiences but is all too often invisible to us. Aristotelian artwork as such lives a kind of double life: it is mimetic or imitative in the Platonic sense, but it is also unique to itself, creating a unique state of affairs set apart from mundane life. This uniqueness enables art to function as a social cathartic for Aristotle, particularly as it relates to tragedies. By enacting the very worst possible human crimes—incest, matricide, murder—the theater can in fact purge us of these drives in a process that Aristotle identified as *catharsis* or cleansing.

The dramatic portrayal of new creation in the drama of the liturgy reconstituted space and time according to the micro-macro relationships inherent in the cosmic order, which enabled the worshipers to commune with the Beauty of the cosmic order while at the same time realizing that order in their liturgical embodiment.

This representational significance of drama is precisely the justification appealed to by the early Christian writer Tatian, a student of Justin Martyr, in his denunciation of Attic theater. Because performances are mimetic, that is, imitative or representative of the world around us, they have a tremendous power in shaping our perception of the world as it was understood in pagan terms. Thus, while early

Christians were generally ascetic in terms of the theater, they turned toward the dramatic portrayal of the new creation in Christ in the eschatological drama of the liturgy. In fact, in the Byzantine East, the liturgy required a form of church interior very similar to the Greek theater: the altar was placed behind a screen pierced with three doors for the priest and deacons, corresponding to the fixed number of three actors in Greek theater,[29] and the doors were surrounded by the scenery of sacred icons, the iconostasis.

The dramatic portrayal of new creation in the drama of the liturgy reconstituted space and time according to the micro-macro relationships inherent in the cosmic order, which enabled the worshipers to commune with the Beauty of the cosmic order while at the same time realizing that order in their liturgical embodiment. For example, worship took place in churches that were constructed facing east, such that the ascent of human words and song paralleled the rising of the sun, with both cathedral and creation praising God together in anticipation of the new creation. Hence, liturgy was cosmology in its fullest micro-macrocosmic expression.[30]

[T]he liturgy of the mass in the West provided the foundry for the medieval mystery and passion plays, which enacted collectively a representative sampling of biblical history from creation to consummation, thus underscoring the linearity of Christian cosmogony.

29. Paul Kurtz, *The Making of Theatre History* (Englewood Cliffs, NJ: Prentice Hall, 1988), 24.
30. For an extended discussion on the cosmological significance of classical Christian liturgy, see Alexander Schmemann, *Introduction to Liturgical Theology* (Crestwood, NY: St. Vladimir's Seminary Press, 1986); and Stratford Caldecott, *Beauty for Truth's Sake: On the Re-enchantment of Education* (Grand Rapids: Brazos, 2009), 121–134.

Moreover, liturgical life helped to establish a distinctively Christian conception of time and space. The church assembled a calendar that consisted of twelve major feast days (along with more than 150 fast days) over the course of the liturgical year, each punctuated with public processions that characterized medieval festivity and ceremony. As Lilley notes: "The ritual geographies of these holy processions traced through the urban landscape, and traced out in the minds of the participants themselves, the mystical symbolism of urban forms, giving them a wider circulation within medieval society beyond the confines of cloister and court."[31] Furthermore, the liturgy of the mass in the West provided the foundry for the medieval mystery and passion plays, which enacted collectively a representative sampling of biblical history from creation to consummation, thus underscoring the linearity of Christian cosmogony.[32]

Summary

In short, the patristic fathers understood the creation as redeemed in the Incarnation, and the sanctified body as the location for encountering that redeemed creation. Through the healing of the sacraments, the creation proleptically restored in the union of heaven and earth in the Incarnation could be both encountered and appropriated in a life of sensory devotion that anticipated in the present the glorious resurrected body and new creation yet to come. As such, the body, redeemed in the restored ecology of the sacraments, provided the aesthetic framework through which the believer could perceive and thus contemplate the world as a created arena displaying the divine attributes of Truth, Goodness, and Beauty.

---

31. Lilley, "Cities of God," 304.
32. Ibid., 306. On the development of the medieval drama tradition, see O. B. Hardison Jr., *Christian Rite and Christian Drama in the Middle Ages: Essays in the Origin and Early History of Modern Drama* (Baltimore: The Johns Hopkins University Press, 1965).

Redemption of the Senses and the Fine Arts

This practice of the redemption of the senses has of course profound implications for the fine arts in our own time. If our aesthetic sense provides the means by which we know divinely imparted meaning in creation, generating an imaginative sense of the world as a theater of divine wonder and Beauty, then our production and perception of the fine arts will be proportionately wondrous and beautiful. The recovery of classical education has an enormous opportunity, for it has recovered the frames of reference for a truly beautiful art that redeems the senses and prepares us for our resurrection. Music within classical consciousness is the means by which the Beauty of a prefallen created order can be communicated to the imagination, embodying the cosmic order as it was meant to be—and has redemptively become—in the revelation of the infinite, kenotic love of the Trinity in the Incarnation: Visual art embodies a sense of Beauty that draws us into an encounter with the True and the Good, delighting us with a proleptic manifestation of the beatific vision, where heaven and earth come together as one, when God floods the cosmos with His incorruptible glory and life-giving radiance. Poetry re-creates language to radiate the divine similarities embedded in the cosmic order and hidden from our sight. And the culinary arts unify ingredients into a recipe of mathematical proportionality and symmetry that foretastes the messianic banquet yet to come.

It is this vision of art that is our inheritance by right of our baptism; it is this vision of art that beckons us and welcomes us to partake of its splendors and savor its beauties, and in doing so prepares the cosmos for its future transfiguration when Christ returns, when God will be all in all.

Chapter Six
Consecrated Thinking: Scripture and the Moral Imagination

Introduction

Thus far we have seen how Truth, Goodness, and Beauty are part of a network of interrelated cosmic, anthropological, and social frames of reference that were constituent elements of both the classical and Christian worlds. Because each person was thought to be born into a world of divine meaning and purpose, there was an inherent moral obligation to live in such a way that fostered a harmonious relationship with both divinity and humanity. From Plato onward, this cosmic piety was revealed to the human soul through the transcendent values of Truth, Goodness, and Beauty, which in turn forged a distinctively Greek educational project termed *paideia* that had as its goal the fostering of souls that were embodiments of these cosmic values. In terms of the model provided by Plato, this project involved two kinds of purifications: the moral and the intellectual, which Christians appropriated in terms of what we are calling the redemption of the senses and the formation of the moral imagination.

Having developed the redemption of the sense in the previous chapter, it is the formation of the moral imagination that will be the subject of this chapter. I shall develop the meaning of the term *moral imagination* and then relate the imagination to the Greek educational project known as *paideia*, particularly as that project appropriated sacred texts as the foundation for virtue formation. We shall then see the role of Scripture in the formation of early Christian *paideia*, which will serve as the historical backdrop for modeling how Scripture can be appropriated in the Christian classroom today to foster a distinctively biblical moral imagination.

The Moral Imagination

Moral imagination is a term coined by the eighteenth-century British statesman Edmund Burke to denote specifically the integrative role—literally the integrity—of the imagination. The imagination has been given to humans by God to perceive the divinely infused meaning of the cosmos, which provides a moral map of the world by which we might live.[1] The imagination is seen here as the location in the human soul where our intellectual, moral, and aesthetic experiences are integrated into a harmonious whole, such that the totality of our experiences can be synthesized and expressed in a Christ-centered intellectual, moral, and spiritual life.[2]

The imagination has been given to humans by God to perceive the divinely infused meaning of the cosmos, which provides a moral map of the world by which we might live.

The tradition that Burke was drawing from here goes back to the classical world, where there were two basic kinds of knowledge, *sci-*

1. For an enriching exposition on the moral imagination, see Vigen Guroian, *Tending the Heart of Virtue: How Classic Stories Awaken a Child's Moral Imagination* (Oxford: Oxford University Press, 1998).
2. For a highly technical overview of the integrative and aesthetic nature of the imagination, see James K. A. Smith, *Imagining the Kingdom: How Worship Works* (Grand Rapids: Baker Academic, 2013).

entia and *theoria*, or in the Latin *ratio* and *intellectus*. While *scientia* dealt with the act of problem solving, *theoria*, derived from the verb meaning "to see" or "to look," probed the world to gaze at reality itself, that in which all things cohered. We may recall our discussion in chapter 2 on Plato's notion of *theoria* as intellectual purification, which involved the contemplation of the True, the Good, and the Beautiful particularly in mathematics, wherein students could encounter a reality that lies beyond appearances. We may further note the similar distinction that Augustine made between knowledge (*scientia*) and wisdom (*sapientia*), the former entailing familiarity with the temporal world while the latter involves embodying eternal reality. As Andrew Louth has noted, the Latin word used to translate *theoria*—*contemplatio*—originally meant something akin to "what goes on in a temple," "referring to the act of beholding the statue of the divinity enshrined in the temple."[3] This divine notion is similar to Aristotle's understanding of *intellectus* in book 10 of his *Nichomachean Ethics*, which involved understanding the world comparable to way in which the gods perceived it.[4]

Sacred Texts, Scripture, and the Imagination in the Greco-Roman World

In the context of the educational project of *paideia*, the practice of *theoria*, or what we are calling the moral imagination, was inextricably linked to sacred texts. In both the Jewish and the Greco-Roman world, sacred texts functioned as the foundation for education and society. We have already looked at how *paideia* had as its purpose the

3. Andrew Louth, "Theology, Contemplation and the University," *Studies in Christian Ethics* 17 (2004): 73.
4. Ibid., 72.

formation of a particular kind of human, one in which the heroic virtues, the *arête*, embedded particularly in the texts of Homer and Hesiod, were embodied in the hearts and the minds of students. The formative process, the transformation of students into living embodiments of the virtues, was termed *morphosis*, and *morphosis* took place through the practice of *mimesis* (*imitatio*), which provided the means by which the heroism of the past could be practiced and thus embodied in the present.[5]

Furthermore, we observed how the *practice* of these virtues took place in the *polis*, the Greek city-state. The classical idea of *paideia* as an educational ideal did not—and in fact could not—exist in a social vacuum. Since *paideia* was more a process of slow, vegetable-like growth, it required a climate and nutrients by which it might be nurtured and cultivated, which, as Plato taught, the social atmosphere of the *polis* was more than able to provide. The interaction between *paideia* and *polis* developed into a synonymous identification of *paideia* and culture.

> *In the context of the educational project of* paideia, *the practice of* theoria, *or what we are calling the moral imagination, was inextricably linked to sacred texts.*

The work of patristic scholar Frances Young has detailed how this conjunction of sacred text, *mimesis*, *morphosis,* and *polis* provided the foundation for the emergence of a distinctly Christian *paideia*. Young traces the process, following a precedent already established in the synagogue, whereby Christian apologists deliberately subordinated the sacred writings of the Greeks (e.g., Homer, Hesiod) to the philosophical, chronological, and theological primacy of the (devel-

5. Gian Biagio Conte and Glenn W. Most, "Imitation," in Simon Hornblower and Antony Spawforth, eds., *The Oxford Classical Dictionary*, 3rd ed. (Oxford: Oxford University Press, 2003), 749.

oping) Christian Scriptures.[6] This process began with exhortations to a distinctively Christian *paideia*, evident in the earliest sacred texts of Christianity, particularly Ephesians (6:4), Hebrews (12:5), and 2 Timothy (3:14–17), developed through early Christian apologists Justin, Tatian, and Theophilus, and received its most significant development in the thought of John Chrysostom in the Greek East and Augustine in the Latin West. This process was further encouraged by the conception of the gathered people of God as the *ekklesia*, the Greek word for "church." *Ekklesia*, interestingly, was not originally a term associated with religious gatherings, unlike the term *synagogue*, but rather a term that denoted the citizen assemblies of the Greek *polis,* where the latest political, religious, philosophical, literary, and artistic ideas would be discussed. The early Christian conception of the *ekklesia* as the new eschatological *polis*, the "New Jerusalem," provided a natural foundry for the nurturing of a distinct Christian *paideia.*

The Christian metanarrative from creation to consummation, from the primeval Adam to the New Adam, provided an alternative cosmic narrative to those of the classical world by which the totality of life could be understood.

The role of Scripture in shaping the human imagination in early Christian *paideia* was the subject of a 1991 study, *Christianity and the Rhetoric of Empire*, in which Averil Cameron explores how the sacred texts of early Christians provided the foundation of what she calls a "totalizing discourse." In other words, the Christian metanarrative from creation to consummation, from the primeval Adam to the New Adam, provided an alternative cosmic narrative to those of the

6. Frances Young, *Biblical Exegesis and the Formation of Christian Culture* (Peabody, MA: Hendrickson, 1997), 68.

classical world by which the totality of life could be understood.[7] Without this precedent for a totalizing discourse inherent in early Christian writing and speech, Cameron argues, Christianity would never have been a world religion in the fourth and fifth centuries. Thus post-Constantinian Christianity was an outgrowth of Christian discourse from its beginnings. Indeed, Cameron concludes that "if ever there was a case of the construction of reality through text, such a case is provided by early Christianity."[8]

With this brief historical survey in place, we can see the centrality of the Scriptures in the formation of a Christian culture that flowed directly out of the apostolic world, through the early Church fathers, filtering, integrating, assimilating the totality of life into a Christian conception of reality, even sweeping up within it the greatest empire the world had yet witnessed. Scripture provided the symbolic universe out of which the imagination could construct metaphors, analogies, and paradigms by which the totality of Greco-Roman and Jewish experience was synthesized and re-expressed in a Christ-centered intellectual, moral, and spiritual life.

The "Cognized Model" of the Imagination

So what does a Scripturally informed moral imagination look like? It is here that I find anthropologist Roy Rappaport's analysis of cultural meaning systems very helpful in schematizing and organizing how the imagination integrates the sacred text with life experiences.[9] Rappaport developed a model for the organization of cultural meaning

7. See the development in Averil Cameron, *Christianity and the Rhetoric of Empire: The Development of Christian Discourse*, Sather Classical Lectures, vol. 55 (Berkeley: University of California Press, 1991), 47–119.
8. Ibid., 21.
9. Roy Rappaport, *Ritual and Religion in the Making of Humanity* (Cambridge: Cambridge University Press, 1999), 263–276.

systems, which he termed "cognized models," in which he demonstrates that the worldview of a population consists of an architecture of levels and distinctions.

By exploring examples of various metaphors, analogies, and parallels for our students, they can begin the formative process, the morphosis, *of being awakened to seeing the totality of life as an integrative expression of the glory of God.*

There are four levels to a cognized model. At the top of the hierarchy, we have what Rappaport calls "ultimate sacred postulates." These are the unquestionable, nonnegotiable presuppositions or foundational beliefs that inform the totality of one's worldview. Rappaport himself liked to refer to the Hebrew *Shema* as an example of an ultimate sacred postulate, as well as to the early Christian confession of faith "Jesus is Lord." It is on this level, that of ultimate sacred postulates, that we place the Scriptures. These texts are nonnegotiable as far as their holiness, their sanctity, their witness to divine life.

The second level involves what Rappaport refers to as "cosmological axioms," which consist of beliefs concerning the fundamental structures of the universe in relation to the ultimate sacred postulates. So cosmological axioms serve to interpret ecology in relation to divine referents.

The third and fourth levels consist of culture and conduct, respectively. This is where the divinely informed cosmological axioms turn into cultural pursuits and ethical behavior. Classically, culture was an idealized reflection of the divinely infused meaning inherent in the created order and provided the tangible substantiation of that meaning in order to draw humanity into communion with divine life and thus conform ethical life accordingly. So it is at these last two levels where cosmology transforms into culture and conduct.

Now, with both the role of the classical canon in *paideia* and this model of the cognized imagination in place, I want to illustrate how the symbolic universe of students can be shaped with biblical images. This involves teaching the student's imagination to see the world anew, mediated through the symbolic world of the Scriptures. By exploring examples of various metaphors, analogies, and parallels for our students, they can begin the formative process, the *morphosis*, of being awakened to seeing the totality of life as an integrative expression of the glory of God.

Ultimate Sacred Postulates

In accordance with both our historical and our anthropological models, Scripture occupies the position of the classical canon constituted by ultimate sacred postulates. What I try to do at this level is to cast all the characters and events of Scripture into what Andrew Louth calls a "synthetic vision" of the dawning of the new creation in Christ.[10] The principle operative here is that all things flow from God through Christ as He embodies the new creation, the bringing together of heaven and earth. From this vantage point, the new creation is inextricably linked—indeed, embodied—by the mystery of Christ, and thus the whole of Scripture is related to that mystery, as per the Pauline contrast between the two Adams in Romans 5:12–21. For example, when reading the David and Goliath narrative, we examine the symbolic universe that constitutes the narrative and see how it coalesces into a vision of the new creation in Christ. Note the parallels to Christ and the Church: David is a shepherd from Bethlehem, armed with garden utensils, who like Joshua (*Yeshua*) is a conqueror of giants and who, by slaying the giant, is then seated

10. Andrew Louth, *Discerning the Mystery: An Essay on the Nature of Theology* (Oxford: Clarendon Press, 1983), 121.

on the throne of God's holy mountain, anointed as God's son and guardian of His bride, Israel. This is a simple example of how the symbolic universe of the narrative constitutes a vision of Christ and His Church. So, the lives of Adam, Abraham, Joseph, Joshua, David, Daniel et al are examined as synthetic visions of Christ and the new creation.[11]

Cosmological Axioms

Scripture provides the symbolic world into which the cosmos is swept, and that brings us to the next level in the cognized model: cosmological axioms. The goal here is to interpret our ecology in relation to that synthetic vision of Christ by teaching students to draw analogies and metaphors between the arena of creation and the divine images of Scripture. The following are some examples of cosmological axioms in Scripture.

The goal here is to interpret our ecology in relation to that synthetic vision of Christ by teaching students to draw analogies and metaphors between the arena of creation and the divine images of Scripture.

The Sun

The sun is a classic symbol of Christ in Christian typology. In the closing prophetic book of the Old Testament, Malachi, we read that for those who fear the name of the Lord, "the sun of righteousness will

11. There are a number of rich resources for interpreting Scripture as a synthetic vision of Christ. See, for example, Peter J. Leithart, *A House for My Name: A Survey of the Old Testament* (Moscow, ID: Canon Press, 2000); James B. Jordan, *Through New Eyes: Developing a Biblical View of the World* (Eugene, OR: Wipf & Stock, 1999); and Vern S. Poythress, *The Shadow of Christ in the Law of Moses* (Phillipsburg, NJ: P & R, 1995).

rise with healing in its wings" (4:2). The sun of course is the "light of the world" that rules the day in parallel to Christ's own self-description. It is set in the blueness of the sky, which is symbolic of the throne room of God.

However, the Christological significance of the sun can be itself *illuminated* by the significance of directionality in the Scriptures. Again, this is the process of drawing analogies in the imagination. We find, particularly in Genesis 1–11, that movement eastward is a movement *away* from the presence of God. When Adam and Eve are cast out of the Garden, God stations cherubim at the east of the Garden to guard the Tree of Life. To get back into the Garden requires traveling west, through the gate set up on the east end. The movement of humanity throughout Genesis 1–11 is eastward, moving further away from the presence of God, climaxing at Babel. The theological significance of the call of Abraham is underscored by the fact that he is the first person to travel west. When the people of God are brought out of Egypt, they do not enter the Promised Land from the south, which would be the natural direction, but instead they travel down and around the Sinai Peninsula up to Moab, where they cross the Jordan River, moving westward into the Promised Land. In fact, when the people of God centuries later are cast out of the land of Israel and sent into exile, they are cast out east toward Babylon, the place of Babel. In their hope of salvation through the coming of the Messiah, it was believed that the Messiah would be coming from the east, moving west through the uninhabitable desert wilderness, through the Jordan River, and climaxing in the Temple to usher in the new heavens and the new earth, as per Malachi 3:1 and Isaiah 40:1–3. If this is the case, if movement from east to west is a movement toward the presence of God, then what does the sun—by rising in the east, passing through the sky, and setting in the west—say to the world every single day? The sun, the symbol of Christ, calls the world to return to God. In fact, second-century theologian Melito of Sardis talked of the fact that every evening the sun appears to descend into the ocean, from which it comes up exultantly, rising as a new sun, "purified from the bath."[12] For Melito, *the setting and the rising* of the sun every day is a call to Christian baptism, which he explicitly linked with Christ's own baptism in the Jordan.

If movement from east to west is a movement toward the presence of God, then what does the sun—by rising in the east, passing through the sky, and setting in the west—say to the world every single day? The sun, the symbol of Christ, calls the world to return to God.

So here we have a cosmological axiom, the sun, informed by the ultimate sacred postulates of the Scriptures, integrated and stored in the memory of the imagination that in turn generates new and profound analogies and metaphors. Students will never look at the sun the same way again.

Mountains

What are mountains in the Scriptures? Mountains are where heaven and earth meet. The downward flow of the rivers of the Garden implies that the Garden is set on a mountainside. The Law of God is received on Mount Sinai; Jerusalem, the city of God, is on Mount Zion; Christ preaches the most famous of sermons on a mount; Christ dies on the hill of Golgatha; in Matthew 28, the resurrected Christ gives the Great Commission on a mountain in Galilee; the Messianic banquet takes place on a holy mountain in Isaiah 25. Furthermore, the stories of the tower of Babel, the pyramids of Pharaoh, and the "seven hills" of Rome should be read as humanity's attempts to bridge heaven and earth by the creation of

12. Killian McDonnell, *The Baptism of Jesus in the Jordan: The Trinitarian and Cosmic Order of Salvation* (Collegeville, MN: Liturgical Press, 1996), 50–51.

our own mountains. Mountains are symbols that heaven and earth will one day come together, and the fact that we already, according to Hebrews, approach the true Mount Zion in our worship is indicative of the fact that heaven and earth have already come together in Christ (Hebrews 12:22).

Trees

We open up the Bible and read about a Garden, and we are told of two very special trees—the Tree of Life and the Tree of the Knowledge of Good and Evil, both of which are in the presence of God. Hence, God's presence is related to trees throughout Scripture. The burning bush narrative; Moses's staff becoming a manifestation of the same glory presence that he saw at the burning bush; the budding of Aaron's rod as the priest of the new Garden; the Solomonic Temple (the dwelling place of the presence of God) made of cedar wood (1 Kings 6); Jesus's coming from the shoot of Jesse and dying on the tree of the cross—we fall at a tree, and we are redeemed at a tree. As a result, God's people can be replanted and flourish "like a tree firmly planted by streams of water,/ Which yields it fruit in its season/ And its leaf does not wither" (Psalm 1:3, NASB). Revelation ends with the restoration of the Tree of Life for the healing of the nations (Revelation 22:2).

Every Christmas, Christians set up trees in their homes, a practice that has its origins in the combination of the medieval paradise tree and the Christmas candle, both of which celebrated the glory and Beauty of the nativity of Christ, who is the new Tree of Life. In the Byzantine tradition, autumn marks the celebration of the Feast of the Exaltation of the Cross. The feast is in the fall because this is when trees lose their leaves, the signs of life, and begin to bear the attributes of crosses. But of course those same trees, in the spring, blossom forth as trees of life at the time of Easter.[13]

---

13. For a beautiful exposition of gardening, ecology, and the liturgical calendar, see Vigen Guroian, *Inheriting Paradise: Meditations on Gardening* (Grand Rapids: Eerdmans, 1999).

Food

Another prominent motif in Scripture is food. God provides food for Adam and Eve in the Garden, for the people of God in the wilderness, for David, for Elijah; Christ feeds the five thousand and refers to Himself as the Bread of Life; Christ initiates the Eucharist, the Lord's Supper, which is a foretaste of the climactic, eschatological, messianic banquet. Note, too, that food is linked with ethics in Scripture. The first commandment that God gave to Adam involved food. In fact, the rabbis saw all 613 commandments summed up in the one command "Do not eat." The reason is that they understood the command as a command against coveting, and they had noticed that the Ten Commandments, the summary of the law, are bookended with commands against coveting. Note further that in Exodus 16, God feeds Israel manna in the wilderness *one day at a time* (Exodus 16:4–5, 12). Why would He do this? The key verse here is Exodus 16:4—God does it this way so that He "may prove them, whether they will walk in [his] law or not." In other words, food is a tangible substantiation of God's call for His people to trust in His promises and provisions. Thus, every meal that we sit down to is a tangible reminder of how God provides for our lives every passing second, a substantial embodiment of His love for us and His unswerving commitment to meet our needs in Christ. In fact, the bread and wine of the Eucharist are rooted in the Genesis creation narrative, in which the earth brings forth grain and fruit, which when processed become bread and wine. Thus the food of the Eucharist, offered as tokens of new creation, is a symbol of the renewal of the entire cosmos in Christ.

Every meal that we sit down to is a tangible reminder of how God provides for our lives every passing second, a substantial embodiment of His love for us and His unswerving commitment to meet our needs in Christ.

Birds

One of my favorite examples of ecological typology comes from the Greek patristic father Saint Ephrem and his interpretation of a bird. He wrote:

> A bird grows up in three stages
> From womb to egg, then to the nest where it sings;
> And once it is fully grown it flies in the air,
> Opening its wings in the symbol of the Cross.
> But if the bird gathers its wings,
> Thus denying the extended symbol of the Cross,
> Then the air too will deny the bird:
> The air will not carry the bird
> *Unless its wings confess the Cross.*[14]

The whole earth is filled with divine images to which we need to awaken our students. The stars in the sky signify the promise to Abraham's heirs of rule and dominion over the earth, while blades of grass are a reminder of the frailty and fleetingness of our lives; rivers are the residue of the original Garden rivers, while the oceans are chaos kept at bay by God's sovereign hand. The wind is the breath of God that is the animating source of life in the cosmos, and our safely falling asleep at night is the care God promises to our souls in death. The planting of the seed in the ground is our return to the dust, and blossoming flowers are the sacred scent of our resurrection.

Culture

As we observed above, Frances Young has demonstrated that the emergence of Christian *paideia* was itself an expression of the cultural significance of the Scriptures for the early Church. Indeed, *paideia* eventually became synonymous with the Latin *cultura*. Again recalling

14. Quoted in Young, *Biblical Exegesis*, 148.

our discussion above, culture or *paideia* in the classical world entailed the reconstitution of time and space around our cosmic piety, our divine obligations, and thus enabled us to fulfill our divine purpose and thereby become truly human. So whether one is dealing with the study of history, art, literature, math, economics, music, or science, all of these constituents were considered tangible material expressions of divine meaning and purpose that we are called to embody and thereby orient our lives in accordance with cosmic virtue. As space does not allow for an exploration of all curricular subjects, I will touch on a representative sample.

Culture or paideia *in the classical world entailed the reconstitution of time and space around our cosmic piety, our divine obligations, and thus enabled us to fulfill our divine purpose and thereby become truly human.*

Music and Mathematics

In our exploration of the redemption of the senses above, I mentioned the Pythagorean concept of the music of the spheres. By tradition, Pythagoras believed that numbers were the key to the universe, and so when he discovered that musical pitches constituted exact numerical ratios, he concluded that the cosmos was indeed held together by music. Music was simply numbers, the key to the symmetrical constitution of the universe, made audible. And because we have access to the math of the universe, we are able to reproduce on earth the music that sounds throughout the heavens, thereby reconstituting humanity as heavenly beings.[15]

15. See Kenneth Sylvan Guthrie, *The Pythagorean Sourcebook and Library: An Anthology of Ancient Writings Which Relate to Pythagoras and Pythagorean Philosophy* (Grand Rapids: Phanes, 1987).

Christian apologists such as Clement of Alexandria reshaped the Pythagorean concept of the music of the spheres by presenting Christ as "the minstrel who imparts harmony to the universe and makes music to God."[16] The symphony of the cosmos is in fact Christ, the *Logos*, in whom all things hold together. Augustine developed this even further in his *De Musica* with the conception that the numbers of music derive from the unchanging order of "eternal numbers," which themselves proceed from God. And it all came together with Boethius in the early sixth century, whose theory of music is structured according the threefold pattern of music of the spheres, music of the natural world, and music of the soul.

> *Because we have access to the math of the universe, we are able to reproduce on earth the music that sounds throughout the heavens, thereby reconstituting humanity as heavenly beings.*

What seems particularly profound is the way music reflects the pattern of redemptive history. Theologian and musician Jeremy Begbie has observed that tonal music operates to a large degree according to teleological principles, that is, musical tones and harmonies rhythmically relate to one another in such a way that we have a sense that the music is going somewhere, that it has a destination, leading us to some kind of goal or "gathering together" of the whole temporal process.[17] This teleological dynamic is generated primarily through a temporal structure that might best be described as equilibrium-tension-resolution. A song begins at a tonal *home*, what we call the *key*, and then the music *departs*, it goes on a journey, and that journey is marked by a kind of *tension*, which

16. Avery Cardinal Dulles, *A History of Apologetics* (Eugene, OR: Wipf and Stock, 1997), 39–40.
17. Jeremy S. Begbie, *Theology, Music and Time* (Cambridge: Cambridge University Press, 2000), 38.

arises from the dissonance of sensing that we are far away from home. But tonal music will always *resolve* that tension by bringing us back home, back to where we belong.

Now we can see therefore that every song in a sense is reflective of the biblical redemptive drama. We begin in the Garden, which is our home, the equilibrium between heaven and earth. In our fall, we are cast out of the Garden, so that that equilibrium between heaven and earth transforms into a dissonance, a disruption, a tension that exists between God and man. But this tension, this dissonance, is then resolved partially by Israel and fully in the coming of the Messiah, who embodies within Himself the equilibrium of heaven and earth brought together once and for all, and so now we can come home again.

Literature

This chiastic structure of equilibrium, tension, and resolution crosses over into the world of literature, where stories can be read in light of the biblical drama, drawing metaphoric and paradigmatic relationships with life experiences. G. K. Chesterton observed that we read the *Iliad* because life is a battle, the *Odyssey* because life is a journey, the book of Job because life is a riddle.[18] In reading Horace, Virgil, or Ovid, students encounter an alternative eschatological vision for the world, with extraordinarily moving poetic celebrations of the reign of Caesar and the glory of Rome. Hence we learn how Paul could contrast the lordship of Caesar with the lordship of the resurrected Christ, which stretches over the entire cosmos and all that is in it, both in heaven and on earth (Romans 1:1–7; cf. Ephesians 1:20–21).[19] From Augustine's *Confessions*, in which every sentence is a prayer to God, we encounter how the prayers of his dear mother for him transform through this book to become Augustine's prayers for us. From Dante, we encounter the beatific vision,

18. G. K. Chesterton, *The Defendant* (London: J. M. Dent, 1907), 47.
19. See, for example, N. T. Wright, "Paul's Gospel and Caesar's Empire," Center of Theological Inquiry public lecture, available at http://ntwrightpage.com/Wright_Paul_Caesar_Empire.pdf.

in which the poet finally captures a glimpse of the wonder and glory of God, as "the love which moves the sun and the other stars." From Shakespeare, we get a foretaste of the banquet accompanying this beatific vision in the redemptive world of comedy.

One of the fundamental differences between the God of the Bible and the divine conceptions of other religions, particularly Eastern religion, is that the God of the Bible reveals Himself in history.

Furthermore, we can take this cognized model we have been using and with it begin to analyze the inner world of stories we read. We can ask of a book: What are its key values, its ultimate sacred postulates? How does it understand Truth, Goodness, and Beauty? How does it understand its cosmos in relation to those key values, and how does that cosmology inform the cultural and ethical life of the characters in the book? So our cognized model becomes a very useful heuristic tool by which to ask the text integrative questions that can then be compared and contrasted with the biblical world.

History

Scripture also profoundly informs our conceptions of history in relation to Truth. One of the fundamental differences between the God of the Bible and the divine conceptions of other religions, particularly Eastern religion, is that the God of the Bible reveals Himself in history. Most other divine encounters are at the level of the private psychological processes, the level of introspection and intuition. This is why meditation, not prayer, is so important for Eastern religions. But the God of the Bible is very different. He is the God of Abraham, Isaac, and Jacob; He is the God who rescues His people from Egypt into the Promised Land; He is the God who has revealed Himself in the transformative life, death, and resurrection of Christ, without which there would never have been a Church. And because God is a God of history and not private introspection, He therefore yields a truth that is every bit as objective as the historical events to which that truth is wedded. Hence, there is a distinctly Christian relationship between history and truth.[20]

Conduct

Finally, from a synthetic vision of Christ and cosmological axioms and culture, we move to conduct, to the ethical life of students. We will explore the ethical life with a passage from Scripture that integrates all the levels of our cognized model.

A person embodying the ethics of a biblically informed moral imagination trusts in the promises and provisions of God through Christ and is thus free to view the needs of others as more important than his or her own.

In Romans 14, Paul exhorted the congregation to accept the one who is weak in faith, the one who is concerned particularly about "food." Paul's rationale, his concern for the weaker brother, was that the gift of the Spirit as the manifestation of the new creation in the present means that Christians, whether weak or strong, enjoy the same relationship with God as humanity enjoyed in the Garden. Hence when they receive their "food" or honor their respective "days" with thanksgiving, glorifying God as the all-sufficient pro-

---

20. For developments of the relationship between God and history, see Ben House, *Punic Wars and Culture Wars: Christian Essays on History and Teaching* (Nacogdoches, TX: Covenant Media Press, 2008); and David F. Wells, *No Place for Truth: Or Whatever Happened to Evangelical Theology?* (Grand Rapids: Eerdmans, 1993), 258–282.

vider for all their needs, they are rendered clean as part of the new creation.[21] What concerned Paul was that members of the congregation can cause the weaker brother to "stumble" by causing him to eat what he considers sinful, even though it is not. For Paul, to do so is to cause the weaker brother to receive food that he cannot in good conscience receive with thanksgiving, that is, he cannot receive it as from the Lord, and thereby eating recapitulates the same attitude that was present at the Fall.

This complex of thought may be termed "Eucharistic ethics": our ethical life is marked by Spirit-endowed trust in the promises and provisions of God, and hence we do all things in thanksgiving, whether we eat or drink, giving glory to God (1 Corinthians 10:31).[22] We don't steal because we trust that God will provide for us. We don't covet after other gods because we trust that God can meet our needs. We don't covet our neighbor's goods because trusting in God to meet our needs frees us to be concerned about the needs of our neighbor. A person embodying the ethics of a biblically informed moral imagination trusts in the promises and provisions of God through Christ and is thus free to view the needs of others as more important than his or her own, embodying the very mind of Christ (cf. Philippians 2:6–11). Hence, Paul drew together divine, cosmological, and cultural frames of reference that inform a distinctively Christian ethic that seeks to foster a life of faith and communion in the promises and provisions of God.

---

21. Scott J. Hafemann, "Eschatology and Ethics: The Future of Israel and the Nations in Romans 15:1–13," *Tyndale Bulletin* 51 (2000): 168–169.
22. Law obedience as an expression of trusting in the promises and provisions of God is most insightfully developed in Scott J. Hafemann, *The God of Promise and the Life of Faith: Understanding of the Heart of the Bible* (Wheaton, IL: Crossway, 2001).

Summary

We have thus seen how the fostering of the moral imagination in students involves cultivating the imagination as the integrative center for the logical, moral, and aesthetic dimensions of life. The Greek educational project of *paideia* took the imagination quite seriously by teaching students to embody the virtues embedded in the sacred texts that comprised the classical canon. As early Christians shaped their own classical canon, which involved relativizing the works of Homer and Hesiod to the Scriptures, they fostered their own *paideia* project that enculturated people into a totalizing discourse that encompassed the manifold constituents of cosmic, cultural, and ethical life. Based on the cultural anthropological model of Roy Rappaport, we explored how a comparable biblical imagination could be fostered in the life of our own students, one that reflects the glory and splendor of God in all things.

CHAPTER SEVEN
Educational Aesthetics: Teaching Truth, Goodness, and Beauty

INTRODUCTION

Having presented a historical overview of Truth, Goodness, and Beauty, and the twin processes of their appropriation—the redemption of the senses and the cultivation of a moral imagination—we are now in a position to reflect on how all of this relates to teaching. If Truth, Goodness, and Beauty are ultimately about drawing students into an encounter with the Holy Trinity through the incorporation of the entire cosmos into the transformative life, death, and resurrection of Christ, then we need to begin to probe our teaching to determine the extent to which our pedagogy entails the constituent elements of Truth, Goodness, and Beauty. This pedagogical inspection would at the very least involve inquiries such as:

- How do we begin meeting our students where they are and awakening them to a world of awe and wonder?
- How do we get our students to see themselves as microcosms of a larger macrocosmic world filled with meaning and obligation?
- If students were created to be drawn to Truth, Goodness, and Beauty, then where is the fostering of a sense of intellectual *eros*, an ardent desire, in our pedagogy?

- How do we refine and order the senses to love what is truly lovely?
- How do we inspire our students to contemplate Truth, Goodness, and Beauty?

In what follows, I want to provide an overview of the classical role of wonder in the knowing process, and then enlist the help of aesthetic theory to provide us with a launching pad for teaching Truth, Goodness, and Beauty. Aesthetic theory can help us to think through and experience how seemingly ordinary things can transform into extraordinary realities. It is my hope that by exploring the various ways in which such transformations take place, the teacher can initiate the process of fostering a new perspective within students, one that begins to see the world anew in Christ, thus enabling our students to respond to that divine invitation whereby they may experience the awakening of the fullness of their humanity.

Awakening Wonder

For Plato, knowledge is rooted in what he considered a kind of intellectual *eros*, a cognitive desire to encounter the world as a reflection of divine life. Or as Socrates declared in Plato's *Theaetetus*: "Philosophy begins in wonder and Iris [who is the messenger of heaven] is the child of wonder [*Thauman*]."[1] According to Aristotle, wonder stimulates all thought and defines best why we freely seek to know the world and its causes. In his *Metaphysics* Aristotle wrote: "It is owing to their wonder that men both now begin and at first began to philosophize."[2] In the words of humanities professor Richard Harp: "The classical tradition regarded wonder as both the origin and permanent companion of all rational inquiry. Wonder . . . was

1. Plato, *Theaetetus*, ed. and trans. by H. N. Fowler, Loeb Classical Library (Cambridge: Harvard University Press, 1921), 155d.
2. Aristotle, *Metaphysics* 982b.

. . . considered a truly rational movement of the mind towards fresh knowledge."[3]

Aesthetic theory can help us to think through and experience how seemingly ordinary things can transform into extraordinary realities.

In contrast to our modern infatuation with self-esteem, it was classically understood that wonder began with an admission of personal impoverishment, what the Greeks called *aporia* and the Latins *pietas*. This in fact is the rationale for the Socratic dialogue; Socrates was able to impart wisdom only when his interlocutor admitted ignorance and perplexity. This intellectual and spiritual vacuousness, this virtue of humility, can then be *filled*, and filled not merely with facts that correspond to purposeless natural or social processes of cause and effect, but with a knowledge of the world as it relates to what is eternally True, Good, and Beautiful. As we saw earlier, Plato in his *Timeaus* proposed that the contemplation of the cosmos could lead the soul to God and hence transcend the cosmos, a concept echoed in Aristotle's *De Philosophia*. This is because, for the classical tradition, the world and the cosmos were what is called in theology "diaphanous," that is, all of creation is a temporal reflection of the eternal Beauty of the divine. And it was the role of culture to provide substantial, palpable, material manifestations of divine reality embedded in the cosmic order. Hence philosophy, history, logic, dialectic, rhetoric, aesthetics, physics, epic, lyric, comedy, democracy (all Greek words!) were means by which one could tangibly encounter *telos*, the divinely infused meaning and purpose embedded in the created order. And education, *paideia* in the Greek world, was precisely the initiation into this culture, for it is through embodying Greek culture that one was able to encounter divine life.

---

3. Richard L. Harp, "*The Winter's Tale*: An 'Old Tale' Begetting Wonder," *Dalhousie Review* 58 (1978): 295.

As an extension of *paideia*, Greco-Roman classical education understood each subject in what was termed the *trivium* and *quadrivium* as a subsidiary means, an instrumental portal if you will, that enabled one to encounter realities that were not specific to any single time or place precisely because they were eternal and divine.[4] The septet of liberal arts was inextricably bound to a diaphanous world, a creation that manifested temporally and spatially God's eternal Beauty, since the whole purpose of the *trivium* and *quadrivium* was to provide lenses through which students could see this divine splendor in creation and hence cultivate a sense of their place in the cosmos. And because the world reflected an eternal dimension, the classical mind recognized, as Andrew Louth notes, that true wisdom is beyond the grasp of the finite creature, man, and is indeed the possession of the gods. Knowledge in its traditional sense begins in wonder and in fact ends in wonder, since one is penetrating more deeply into the mystery of reality. Hence the term *philosophia*: the "love of wisdom." Impelled by this love for wisdom, Josef Pieper comments, "Wonder is not just the starting point of philosophy in the sense of *initium*, of a prelude or preface. Wonder is the *principium*, the lasting source, the *fons et origo*, the immanent origin of philosophy. . . . The inner form of philosophizing is virtually identical with the inner form of wonder."[5]

For the classical tradition, the world and the cosmos were what is called in theology "diaphanous," that is, all of creation is a temporal reflection of the eternal Beauty of the divine.

4. For an excellent overview of the seven liberal arts, see Kevin Clark and Ravi Jain, *The Liberal Arts Tradition: A Philosophy of Christian Education* (Camp Hill, PA: Classical Academic Press, 2013).
5. Quoted in Andrew Louth, *Discerning the Mystery*, 144.

Aesthetic Knowledge

But *how* do we get our students to see this world of wonder and awe? It is here that I believe familiarity with the field of aesthetics can be of great benefit. Aesthetics is based on the Greek verb *aisthanomai*, meaning "sense perception" or "to apprehend by means of the senses," and appears to have been first used by German philosopher Alexander Baumgarten (1714–1762) in his 1750 tract *Aesthetica*. Baumgarten was interested particularly in deducing the rules or principles of artistic and natural Beauty. The term developed as a species of philosophy that involved an inquiry into the nature of art and Beauty.[6] However, I am more interested in the classical conception of art, which viewed art as a form of *communication*. In this sense, art reveals the nature and meaning of reality to the observer in order to generate certain desirable dispositions or virtues.[7] It is by discerning the various ways in which art communicates that we can teach students to begin to probe the various constituents of their daily experience as modes of meaning and character formation.

Art reveals the nature and meaning of reality to the observer in order to generate certain desirable dispositions or virtues.

Broadly speaking, there are three schools of thought in aesthetics: *representation*, *formalism*, and *expressionism*. These are three ways of characterizing or describing art, of observing the processes and characteristics by which art functions in our world and manifests meaning to our senses. In what follows, I will apply each school of aesthetic thought as a template through which students can see anew

6. See the overview in Dabney Townsend, *Aesthetics: Classical Readings from the Western Tradition*, 2nd ed. (Belmont, CA: Wadsworth/Thompson Learning, 2001).
7. Richard Viladesau, *Theological Aesthetics: God in Imagination, Beauty, and Art* (Oxford: Oxford University Press, 1999), 9.

classical Christian subject matter, such that each subject transforms into a portal of wider meaning. Training students to see the world *through* the curricular subject is crucial to awakening their senses and imaginations to the divine meaning inherent in the cosmos and redeemed in Christ.

Representation: Embodying the Invisible

The first school of thought is *representation*. Representation sees art basically functioning as a mode of metaphor. When someone makes the statement, "This rose is my love for you," what is happening there? The rose is presented not *merely* as a rose, but as a tangible expression, a concrete manifestation, of the person's love. The rose represents, literally *re*presents, substantially something that otherwise would have been abstract and impalpable, namely, "love." This is representation: art represents an impalpable, intangible, abstract reality in palpable, tangible, concrete terms. And in so doing, it transforms the object of representation; the rose in our example is no longer *merely* a rose; it is embodies an idea, an expression that transforms its significance, in that its connotations are widened in the metaphor.

Numbers point beyond themselves to something that awakens awe and wonder within us. We begin to discover meaning through numbers.

Why are we attracted to metaphor? What's the Beauty in metaphor, and why does metaphor communicate delight? I think the philosopher Michael Polanyi was correct in noticing that metaphor exemplifies the way we know the world.[8] We all look at the world through *subsidiary* means that draw us to a *focal* point. So I look at the world *through* my eyes; my eyes provide the subsidiary means by which I can focus on something beyond my eyes. If I start looking at my eyes, going cross-eyed, as it were, I lose focus. The only way I see the world is through something that allows me to see. I think this is why we take delight in metaphor; metaphors in a sense become a new set of eyes through which we can "see" the meaning infused in creation.

Now, with regard to school subjects, art functioning as metaphor of course has direct parallels with the world of literature. We "see" through stories when we see that they point beyond themselves to a larger story, that they are microcosms of a larger narrative macrocosm.[9] Whether we are dealing with children's literature or Shakespeare, stories give us a taste of the meaning of our world through the narrative world. Thus, Shakespeare's tragedies are seen to represent the Fall of humanity, and his comedies represent our redemption; *Sleeping Beauty* can be seen as a story about a Christ-redeemer who slays a dragon and rescues his betrothed by raising her to life. In *Pinocchio*, the hardened wood represents laziness, lying, and self-centeredness, and the puppet's transformation into a human represents the divine processes of regeneration and transfiguration. The *Little Mermaid* represents the quest for eternal life; *Charlotte's Web* represents life as communion and friendship.[10]

Along with awakening students to life through the world of literature, representation can illumine mathematics. The Greeks, following the Pythagorean school of thought, noticed that numbers do not exist in time and space. No one has ever seen the number "one," for

8. Michael Polanyi, *The Tacit Dimension.*
9. On discerning meaning in literature and art, see Gregory Wolfe, *Beauty Will Save the World: Recovering the Human in an Ideological Age* (Wilmington, DE: Intercollegiate Studies Institute, 2011).
10. For an exposition of the broader themes inherent in fairy tales, see Vigen Guroian, *Tending the Heart of Virtue: How Classic Stories Awaken a Child's Moral Imagination* (Oxford: Oxford University Press, 1998).

example; none of us has bumped into the number "one"; no one has heard or smelled it, etc. This is because the number "one" does not extend in time and space; it appears only as an adjective: one pencil, one book, one student. But the Greeks asked, What would happen to human civilization if we said that numbers and mathematics don't actually exist? We couldn't build bridges, or buildings, or roads, or anything; the regularity of the universe would be called into question; everything would collapse. So our existence, our experience of numbers, is testimony to the fact that numbers and mathematics must exist, *but they must exist in another world.* And because mathematics deals with a perfect world, then it must be a divine world. So mathematics represents, literally *re*presents, that divine world in this one, and thus every time I do mathematics I am communing with divine life, or in Augustine's refinement, the architecture of a divine mind. Via representation, numbers are not just numbers. They point beyond themselves to something that awakens awe and wonder within us. We begin to discover *meaning* through numbers.

By looking at our subjects through the lens of the aesthetic theory of representation, our subject matter transforms into a new set of eyes through which our students can begin to see the meaning inherent in the created order.

Hence the mystical nature of numbers for the Greeks and early Christians: the eternal generation of numbers accounts for the order and the symmetry of the cosmos. This order and symmetry is demonstrated in binaries: God/man, heaven/earth, good/evil, life/death, hot/cold, man/woman, light/darkness, and all the binaries of the cosmos are numerically represented by the binaries one and zero, which together make the number ten, the *decad*, which represents the cosmos. Hence the most important numbers are one, two, three, four, what they called the *tetraktys*, which when added together not only made up ten but also accounted for the four mathematical dimensions: point, line, plane, and solid. These corresponded to the four elements that made up the cosmos: earth, air, fire, and water; which corresponded to the four Gospels, in which the cosmos is recalibrated around Christ, who is the *Logos*, the one in whom all things hold together. Numbers awaken the meaning of the cosmos to us.[11]

Such meaning made its way into classical Christian architecture and its use of geometric representation. The circular dome represented heaven, with the circle representing eternity; the four corners of the floor represented the four corners of the earth; Byzantine churches in particular were a perfect square, representing the Holy of Holies; often there were four pillars stretching down from the heavenly dome to the earthly floor, which represented the four Gospels testifying that heaven has come down to earth in Christ. And of course, the cruciform became the standard floor plan in the Christian West so that every church was a tangible representation of the world re-created through the cross.[12]

Colors take on representational value as well. Blue signified eternity as per the sky and the ocean depths; white signified purity and rebirth; green represented life; black represented death; red represented love as well as the fire of the Holy Spirit. For example, what color are your school uniforms? Our students are dressed in uniforms that are predominantly blue, and I never tire of reminding them of what blue represents in the classical Christian consciousness; every day, when they put on their uniforms, they should be reminded that they are being prepared for eternity.

Thus, by looking at our subjects through the lens of the aesthetic theory of representation, our subject matter transforms into a new

---

11. See the extended discussion in Stratford Caldecott, *Beauty for Truth's Sake: On the Re-enchantment of Education* (Grand Rapids: Brazos, 2009), 53–87; and Miranda Lundy, "Sacred Number," in John Martineau, ed., *Quadrivium: The Four Classical Liberal Arts of Number, Geometry, Music, and Cosmology* (New York: Walker and Company, 2010), 7–56.
12. Caldecott, *Beauty for Truth's Sake*, 99–104.

set of eyes through which our students can begin to see the meaning inherent in the created order.

Formalism: Order out of Disorder

The second school of aesthetics is *formalism*. Formalism is interested in how art reflects the performance of creating order out of disorder and thus transforming chaos into a controlled display of form and content. A good example of this is the virtuoso instrumentalist, in whose hands the instrument exemplifies extraordinary control in contrast to the cacophony sounding from inexperienced hands.

The creation of order out of disorder in art reflects the very processes of primeval creation in Genesis 1.

However, there is a profound primordial significance to formalism. The creation of order out of disorder in art reflects the very processes of primeval creation in Genesis 1, where we read that the earth was without form and void and are then treated to the processes by which God formed and filled the cosmos. As we noted above, the Septuagint, the ancient Greek translation of the Hebrew Scriptures, explicitly links this creative process with Beauty. In the original Hebrew version of the Genesis creation account, a responsive refrain accompanies each one of God's creative actions: "and it was good." The word there for "good" is the Hebrew *tob*. However, when it was translated into the Greek in the third century before Christ, the translators rendered the term for "good" as *kallos*, which not only means "beautiful" but is related etymologically to *kalein*, "to call," a relationship that had profound significance for the patristic and medieval conceptions of Truth, Goodness, and Beauty.[13]

It is this interpretation of Genesis that inspired both Jewish and Christian traditions to see God as not merely creating a beautiful cosmos out of the chaos but creating it *beautifully*. As such, they conceived of God not merely speaking creation into being but rather singing creation into being. C. S. Lewis had a deep sense of this when he wrote *The Magician's Nephew*, in which Aslan sings the world of Narnia into being, creating Narnia through song. We see a similar symphonic creation of Middle-earth by Eru Ilúvatar in J. R. R. Tolkien's *The Silmarillion*. And because form and content awaken through song, our singing is representative of the very means by which the cosmos comes into being; our *culture* reflects and in fact idealizes our *creation*. So throughout the Old Testament, creation itself is depicted as a great temple in which worship is to be done—God sets the foundations, stretches the heavens as a canopy, and we are here to pick up on that song of creation and make it manifest, make it audible in the world (cf. Psalm 104).[14] We are here to engage in cultural pursuits that make divinely infused meaning of creation palpable so that we can encounter the self-replenishing fountain of Edenic life.

Thus, from Pythagoras (ca. 570–490 BC) to Boethius (AD 480–524), we find that that the entire cosmos is subject to the same laws of proportion that rule music, so that from the inaudible music of the spheres to the proportions of the human body (which is reflected in architecture and art) and the logic of the human soul, all things form a great harmony. Hence, the goal of music is to awaken on earth the music of the heavens; while we can't hear that music (in that we are too far and fallen), we do have access to the mathematics by which that music constantly sounds. This is reflected in the Greek

13. See chapters 3 and 4.
14. Cf. Vigen Guroian, *The Melody of Faith: Theology in an Orthodox Key* (Grand Rapids: Eerdmans, 2010), 2.

word *symmetria*, which means "beautiful." By awakening the music of the heavens on earth through the study of mathematical proportionality and symmetry, we are able to embody such proportionality and symmetry and thus transform into heavenly beings.[15]

In addition to seeing order created out of disorder in creation and in music, we can see similar processes in athletics. Ask your students to imagine what would happen if someone handed a young Michael Jordan a basketball and said to him, "Do whatever you want with it. Do whatever comes to mind. Go ahead and impart your own subjective meaning to the ball!" What would have been the result? Fortunately, Jordan picked up a ball and learned the rules, the boundaries, the order and form of the game, and in so doing great things came alive! This *freeing* aspect of following rules is in fact how G. K. Chesterton thought of Christianity: "The more I considered Christianity, the more I found that while it had established a rule and order, the chief aim of that order was to give room for good things to run wild."[16]

"The more I considered Christianity, the more I found that while it had established a rule and order, the chief aim of that order was to give room for good things to run wild."

Indeed, athletics in the classical world were inextricably linked to the concept of self-mastery (*enkrateia*), the formation of an excellent disposition, which was the key virtue that separated the Greeks from the barbarians. Thus, the language of athletic competition was often used to think about the development of the virtue of self-mastery in

15. For a helpful overview of the classical conception of *harmonia* and its relationship to virtue, see Basil Cole, *Music and Morals: A Theological Appraisal of the Moral and Psychological Effects of Music* (Staten Island, NY: Abba House, 1993), 15–45.
16. G. K. Chesterton, *Orthodoxy* (Garden City, NY: Image Book, 1959), 95.

the life of a philosopher. We see Paul appealing to athletic imagery in 1 Corinthians 9:24–26 as a metaphor for his mastery over passions and temptations, in the context of forgoing his legitimate prerogatives as an apostle for the sake of serving others in the gospel. So athletic competition can be a wonderful embodiment of the Christian life in which one masters a set of rules for the sake of others so that good things run wild.

> *We humans, created in the image of God, are naturally endowed with an attraction to form over chaos; form keeps us away from danger, protects vital life processes, and enables good things to run wild.*

Moreover, the very rules and standards operative in daily school life can be appreciated anew from the vantage point of formalism. I think it is essential that students learn to appreciate that the various practices, acts, arrangements, and etiquettes that organize and govern the life of a school collectively reveal the school as *sacred space*—a place sanctified, set apart from the world as a lived-out expression of a people in but not of the world. However, the formal standards and rules of a school can be a huge stumbling block for both students and parents, and this is largely because both students and parents are tacitly breathing in secular air. Rules in the secular, modern age are by definition arbitrary; we have a tacit understanding that all rules, all laws, are arbitrary and are there only because some people have the power to put them there. It is in light of these secular frames of reference that a school's rules and standards will be naturally interpreted. We as educators have to bring this secular bias to the surface with students. We have to awaken our students to the fact that their cynicism toward rules and standards is derived and sustained by *secular* assumptions. However, by understanding the school as sacred space, students will immediately realize that sacred spaces require special rules, because it is these rules that set school space apart from mundane space. *Special places require special rules.*

So understanding formalism, the means by which order is created out of disorder, enables us to experience the original processes of creation in all areas of our lives and thus actively participate in the new creation. We humans, created in the image of God, are naturally endowed with an attraction to form over chaos; form keeps us away from danger, protects vital life processes, and enables good things to run wild. This is why we love form. And by examining our course curricula in light of how classical Christian education creates order out of disorder through the trivium and quadrivium, we will find that we are engaged in more than just a method of learning subjects; we are engaged in formative processes that enable us to begin to transform the chaos in our own lives and in our own world into formal expressions of Beauty as well.

Expressionism: The Beauty of Community

This last observation leads us to the third school of aesthetics, and that is *expressionism*. Expressionist theories of art share the view that the essence of art is found in how a painting, sculpture, or building is transformed into a perpetual manifestation of human emotion. This theory is consistent with much of our actual talk about art. We often hear of what artists intended to "express" in their artwork; we hear the same thing from critics and art lovers, who seek to understand what an artist is trying to express. But expressionism, particularly in the thought of Leo Tolstoy, sees the artistic embodiment of emotion as a way by which we transcend ourselves and collectively enter into a shared life-world.[17] The feeling of art is a means to *shared* feelings, cre-

17. See the discussion in Townsend, *Aesthetics*, 204–212.

ating community not merely between humans but between humans and God. In short, art in this sense is inherently *communal*; it brings people together for a common purpose and goal.

> *Expressionist theories of art share the view that the essence of art is found in how a painting, sculpture, or building is transformed into a perpetual manifestation of human emotion.*

This communal nature of art is profoundly captured in the choral arts. There is a reason why every political or social movement and every culture is expressed in corporate song. When we sing together, we are not merely claiming to create a social harmony and unity; we are *demonstrating* social harmony. Our collective singing realizes and manifests tangibly in time and space the very Christological unity our hymns profess.

Think further how *time* itself is realigned in our choral singing. We can think of our experience of time in at least four ways.[18] First, there is subjective or individual time, the time I experience as an individual (the time between breaths, the time between heartbeats, the tempo of my speaking, etc.); second, time is experienced socially, representative of our corporate experience of time (time conceived of in terms of breakfast, lunch, dinner, rush hour, Sunday morning worship, Christmas, Thanksgiving). Third, we experience as well a sense of historical time (the time of the Romans, the missionary travels of Paul, the documents of the founding fathers). And finally, we can think of a cosmic sense of time, a time of great epochs and civilizations, the time of creation, the sun, moon, and stars, and even heaven itself.

---

18. I borrow this temporal schema from Roy Rappaport, *Ritual and Religion in the Making of Humanity*, 222–225.

Through the choral arts, these various experiences of time are all drawn together in a communal experience that creates a completely unique sense of time. When we sing together, we are obviously experiencing corporate time; however, we are singing the same song, the same words, the same thoughts, at the same tempo, taking the same breaths, so we are collectively experiencing subjective time; and if we are singing hymns or psalms composed by our spiritual forefathers with tunes of old, we are in fact experiencing historical time; and because of the theological content of our songs, focusing on God and His works, we experience cosmic time.

What we have witnessed here is how the choral arts blend together experiences of time in corporate song in such a way as to manifest a totally unique experience of time, what we can call eschatological time, embodied in a Christ-centered social unity. This is a true expression of Galatians 3:28, "We are all one in Christ Jesus" (author translation); our identity as an eschatological people is profoundly manifested in song, and hence our senses are awakened to a manifestation of eschatological reality. We have just seen how music does in fact re-create the world.

The feeling of art is a means to shared feelings, creating community not merely between humans but between humans and God.

From an expressionist perspective, we are interested in exploring our subjects in terms of how they manifest the Beauty of communion. Note how this relates to the reading of a book: ask your students, Have you ever noticed that a book is completely silent as long as its cover is closed? The author comes alive only when a student opens the book and begins to read. The student awakens the author. However, no two people can read a given book in the exact same way any more than two pianists can play Bach in the exact same way. A book in a very real way awakens a student to realize an experience of him- or herself that would never have happened were it not for those moments of communion with the author.

School uniforms are relevant here as well. School uniforms demonstrate a common *telos*, purpose, or goal. This is the case with *all* uniforms, whether in sports, military, or the clergy; uniforms embody a *shared* identity, a *shared* purpose, and thus our students are encouraged to exercise their individual gifts for the benefit of the whole group, the whole community, to the glory of God. Hence Paul could say to the Galatians, "All of you who have been baptized in Christ have been *clothed* with Christ . . . we are all *one* in Christ" (Galatians 3:27–28, author translation).

Moreover, expressionism can help our students to rethink their understanding of *freedom*. Freedom in the secular conception is often characterized as a negative freedom, a freedom *from*, or subjective freedom, the freedom to follow my heart, to do what I want to do. This view of freedom is derivative of the assumption pervasive in the modern age that we are each born into a world without any divine obligation apart from what I choose to impose upon myself. But in the Christian tradition, freedom is more positive; it is the ability to become what one was created to be, the freedom to fulfill our divine calling. And what our students need to learn to embody is the fact that this freedom in the context of community finds its rationale in terms of Christ's own self-giving, His freely giving Himself up for the life of the world. So Paul said to the Corinthians: "If meat causes my brother to stumble, may I never eat meat again" (1 Corinthians 8:13, author translation). This is Christian freedom: considering the needs of others as more important than my own, trusting all of my needs to God, loving God, loving neighbor, and hence fulfilling the law. So this *freedom to fast*, this voluntary laying down of one's own prerogatives for the sake of others, not only provides a governing rationale for a school's rules and standards but also is a Christ-centered way of getting students to work out their conflicts among themselves in a God-glorifying way, in a way by which they can embody Christ's own self-giving freedom.

By communing with the manifestation of the splendor of God in all our subject matter, students get a glimpse of the ultimate goal of our Christian cultural pursuits . . . when God floods the cosmos with His incorruptible glory and life-giving radiance.

Finally, I think classical education's emphasis on the *integration* of subject matter is absolutely crucial here. Because theology functions as the integrative center through which all course subjects cohere, the totality of life appears to students as a manifestation of the splendor of God. And here we come full circle with the classical conception of Beauty. By communing with the manifestation of the splendor of God in all our subject matter, students get a glimpse of the ultimate goal of our Christian cultural pursuits, what theology calls the beatific vision, the vision of the New Jerusalem in Revelation 22, where heaven and earth come together as one, when God floods the cosmos with His incorruptible glory and life-giving radiance. It is just such a glimpse that can transform students into embodiments of that beatific vision for our world today.

Summary and Epilogue

Now perhaps we have a better idea of how Truth, Goodness, and Beauty can recalibrate our teaching to foster awe and wonder within our students. By awakening our students to Beauty, they encounter that which awakens an *eros*, a desiring wonder and awe, which provides the momentum, the attraction that draws them into communion with the True and the Good, thereby cultivating their intellectual and ethical capacities. Aesthetic theory, summed up in representation, formalism, and expressionism, provides processes by which students learn to contemplate, to see each subject of the classical Christian curriculum transformed into a portal for divine purpose and presence, which in turn causes students to see themselves as microcosmic parts of a wider world of meaning. Each subject in its own way points beyond itself to cosmic realities, *re*presented in the subject itself; each subject exemplifies the processes of the original creation by which God transformed disorder into order, chaos into form; and each subject serves to unite us together in a common purpose of a shared life-world that manifests in the present the beatific vision yet to come. Students thus encounter the manifestation of Truth, Goodness, and Beauty in every area of their lives, sanctifying the senses and imagination alike with a synthetic vision of the glory of God.

The entire object of true education is to make people not merely do the right things, but enjoy the right things.

Thus, we must ask ourselves: Are we presenting music and mathematics, Beauty and symmetry, as inseparable? Do we teach our students to see athletic skill as an embodiment of control over chaos and thus exemplative of the processes of creation? Do our science classes teach that discovery of the workings of the world not only gives us knowledge but awakens us to the awe and wonder of the Incarnation itself? Do our history classes present the totality of history as an eschatological narrative from Garden to city, from creation to communion, from water to wine? Do our Bible classes present theology as rooted in *philokalia*, the love of Beauty? Do we teach our students that there is something extraordinary about the *imagio Dei*, that we yearn for a meaning and a purpose outside of ourselves, that we long for a Beauty that awakens us from our self-centered slumbers, that our hearts ache for a life filled with wonder and awe? Are we cultivating an insatiable desire in our students to encounter the True, the Good, and the Beautiful in a life-transforming way, a way that enables our souls to reach for and embrace a state of being than which none greater can possibly be thought?

In closing, let us recall C. S. Lewis's concern over *The Green Book* and its negative effects on education. Its authors, Gaius and Titius, would have us believe that the purpose of education is to make men masters of method, guardians of utilitarianism and pragmatism, equipped to deconstruct human nature and cultural endeavor as empty social constructs. Yet standing against these dehumanizing tendencies is John Ruskin's aesthetic description of the purpose of education:

> The entire object of true education is to make people not merely do the right things, but enjoy the right things—not merely industrious, but to love industry—not merely learned, but to love knowledge—not merely pure, but to love purity—not merely just, but to hunger and thirst after justice.[19]

Our task as educators is nothing less than to awaken students to the self-replenishing fountain of indescribable delights of a new creation in Christ, to give them the gift of the freedom to be human again, and in so doing to watch their lives blossom into rational, poetic, worshipers of God, and through their lives to get a taste of what life will be like when Christ returns, when God will be all in all. This is our calling, and it is beautiful.

---

19. John Ruskin, *The Crown of Wild Olive: Three Lectures on Work, Traffic, and War* (New York: John Wiley & Sons, 1866), 50.

Bibliography

Primary Sources

Aquinas, Thomas. *Questiones Disputatae de Veritate*. Translated by Robert W. Schmidt. Chicago: Henry Regnery Company, 1954.

———. *Summa Contra Gentiles*. Translated by James F. Anderson. Notre Dame, IN: University of Notre Dame Press, 1975.

———. *Summa Theologica*. Translated by Fathers of the English Dominican Province. New York: Benziger Bros., 1947.

Aristotle. *Metaphysics*. Edited and translated by Hugh Tredennick. 2 vols. Loeb Classical Library. Cambridge: Harvard University Press, 1933-35.

———. *Nicomachean Ethics*. Loeb Classical Library. Cambridge, MA: Harvard University Press, 1994.

———. *The Nichomachean Ethics*. Edited and translated by H. Rackham. Loeb Classical Library. Cambridge: Harvard University Press, 1968.

Athanasius. *On the Incarnation*. Translated by Sister Penelope Lawson. Crestwood, NY: St. Vladimir's Seminary Press, 2002.

Augustine. *City of God, Christian Doctrine. Nicene and Post-Nicene Fathers* 2, edited by Philip Schaff. Peabody, MA: Hendrickson, 2004.

———. *Confessions*. Translated by Henry Chadwick. Oxford: Oxford University Press, 1992.

———. *Confessions*. Translated by Albert C. Outler. Philadelphia: Westminster Press, 1955.

———. *Earlier Writings*. Translated by John H. S. Burleigh. Philadelphia: Westminster, 1953.

———. *The Happy Life, Answer to Skeptics, Divine Providence and the Problem of Evil, Soliloquies*. Translated by Ludwig Schopp. Washington, DC: Catholic University of America Press, 1948.

———. *On the Trinity: Introduction, Translation, and Notes*. Translated by Edmund Hill. Brooklyn: New York City Press, 1991.

Descartes, René. "Meditations on First Philosophy." In *Knowledge and Reality*. Vol. 2 of *First Philosophy: Fundamental Problems and Readings in Philosophy*, edited by Andrew Bailey. Toronto: Broadview Press, 2004.

Ficino, Marsilio. *The Philebus Commentary*. Translated by Michael J. B. Allen. Berkeley: University of California Press, 1975.

Gregory of Nyssa. "Dogmatic Treatises." Translated by William Moore and Henry Austin Wilson. In *Nicene and Post-Nicene Fathers* 5, edited by Philip Schaff. Peabody, MA: Hendrickson, 2004.

———. *The Life of Moses*. Translated by Abraham J. Malherbe and Everett Ferguson. New York: Paulist Press, 1978.

Plato. *Plato in Twelve Volumes*. Vols. 5 and 6. Translated by Paul Shorey. Cambridge, MA: Harvard University Press, 1969.

———. *Plato in Twelve Volumes*. Vol. 9. Translated by Harold N. Fowler. Cambridge, MA: Harvard University Press, 1925.

Pseudo-Dionysius. *The Complete Works*. Translated by Colm Luibheid. New York: Paulist Press, 1987.

Secondary Sources

Aertsen, Jan A. *Medieval Philosophy and the Transcendentals: The Case of Thomas Aquinas*. Leiden: Brill, 1996.

Andreopoulos, Andreas. *Metamorphosis: The Transfiguration in Byzantine Theology and Iconography*. Crestwood, NY: St. Vladimir's Seminary Press, 2005.

Aristotle. *On Rhetoric*. Edited and translated by J. H. Freese. Loeb Classical Library. Cambridge: Harvard University Press, 1926.

Barker, Margaret. *Temple Themes in Christian Worship*. London: T & T Clark, 2007.

Beck, Roger. *The Religion of the Mithras Cult in the Roman Empire: Mysteries of the Unconquered Sun*. Oxford: Oxford University Press, 2006.

Begbie, Jeremy S. *Theology, Music and Time*. Cambridge: Cambridge University Press, 2000.

Beierwaltes, Werner. "The Love of Beauty and the Love of God." In *Classical Mediterranean Spirituality: Egyptian, Greek, Roman*, edited by A. H. Armstrong and A. A. Armstrong, 293–313. *World Spirituality* 15. New York: Crossroads, 1986.

Bertram, Georg. "καλός." In *Theological Dictionary of the New Testament*, edited by Gerhard Kittel et al, 3:536–56. Grand Rapids: Eerdmans, 1977.

Blowers, Paul M. "Maximus the Confessor, Gregory of Nyssa, and the Concept of 'Perpetual Progress.'" *Vigiliae Christianae* 46, no. 2 (June 1992): 151–71.

Bourdieu, Pierre. *Outline of a Theory of Practice.* Translated by Richard Nice. Cambridge: Cambridge University Press, 1977.

Brann, Eva. *The Logos of Heraclitus.* Philadelphia: Paul Dry Books, 2011.

Caldecott, Stratford. *Beauty for Truth's Sake: On the Re-enchantment of Education.* Grand Rapids: Brazos, 2009.

Cameron, Averil. *Christianity and the Rhetoric of Empire: The Development of Christian Discourse.* Sather Classical Lectures 55. Berkeley: University of California Press, 1991.

Chesterton, G. K. *The Defendant.* London: J. M. Dent, 1907.

———. *Orthodoxy.* Garden City, NY: Image Book, 1959.

Clark, Kevin and Ravi Jain. *The Liberal Arts Tradition: A Philosophy of Christian Education.* Camp Hill, PA: Classical Academic Press, 2013.

Cole, Basil. *Music and Morals: A Theological Appraisal of the Moral and Psychological Effects of Music.* Staten Island, NY: Abba House, 1993.

Conte, Gian Biagio, and Glenn W. Most. "Imitation." In *The Oxford Classical Dictionary*, 3rd ed., edited by Simon Hornblower and Antony Spawforth, 749. Oxford: Oxford University Press, 2003.

Cousin, Victor. *Lectures on the true, the beautiful, and the good.* Translated by O. W. Wight. New York: D. Appleton & Co., 1861.

Daniélou, Jean. *Platonisme et théologie mystique.* Paris: Aubier, 1944.

Daniélou, J., and H. Musurillo, eds. *From Glory to Glory: Texts from Gregory of Nyssa's Mystical Writings.* Crestwood, NY: St. Vladimir's Seminary Press, 1995.

Dio Cassius. *Roman History Vol. VI.* Edited and translated by Earnest Cary. Loeb Classical Library. Cambridge: Harvard University Press, 1980.

Douglas, Mary. *Purity and Danger: An Analysis of the Concepts of Pollution and Taboo.* New York: Routledge, 2002.

Dulles, Avery Cardinal. *A History of Apologetics.* Eugene, OR: Wipf and Stock, 1997.

Eco, Umberto. *The Aesthetics of Thomas Aquinas.* Cambridge, MA: Harvard University Press, 1988.

Ephrem the Syrian, *Hymns on Faith,* 81.9. Cited in Susan Ashbrook Harvey, *Scenting Salvation*, 61, 260 n.21.

Festugière, André-Jean. *Le Dieu Cosmique, La Révélation D'Hermès Trismégiste* II. Paris: Librairie Lecoffre, 1949.

———. *Personal Religion among the Greeks.* Berkeley: University of California Press, 1954.

Grundmann, Walter. "ἀγαθός." In *Theological Dictionary of the New Testament,* edited by Gerhard Kittel et al., 1:10–17. Grand Rapids: Eerdmans, 1977.

Guroian, Vigen. *The Melody of Faith: Theology in an Orthodox Key*. Grand Rapids: Eerdmans, 2010.

———. *Inheriting Paradise: Meditations on Gardening*. Grand Rapids: Eerdmans, 1999.

———. *Tending the Heart of Virtue: How Classic Stories Awaken a Child's Moral Imagination*. Oxford: Oxford University Press, 1998.

Guthrie, Kenneth Sylvan. *The Pythagorean Sourcebook and Library: An Anthology of Ancient Writings Which Relate to Pythagoras and Pythagorean Philosophy*. Grand Rapids: Phanes, 1987.

Hafemann, Scott J. *The God of Promise and the Life of Faith: Understanding of the Heart of the Bible*. Wheaton, IL: Crossway, 2001.

———. "Eschatology and Ethics: The Future of Israel and the Nations in Romans 15:1-13." *Tyndale Bulletin* 51 (2000): 168–69.

Hardison, O. B., Jr. *Christian Rite and Christian Drama in the Middle Ages: Essays in the Origin and Early History of Modern Drama*. Baltimore: The Johns Hopkins University Press, 1965.

Harp, Richard L. "*The Winter's Tale*: An 'Old Tale' Begetting Wonder." *Dalhousie Review* 58 (1978): 295–308.

Harrison, Carol. *The Art of Listening in the Early Church*. Oxford: Oxford University Press, 2013.

———. *Beauty and Revelation in the Thought of Saint Augustine*. Oxford: Clarendon Press, 1992.

Hart, David Bentley. *The Beauty of the Infinite: The Aesthetics of Christian Truth*. Grand Rapids: Eerdmans, 2003.

Harvey, Susan Ashbrook. *Scenting Salvation: Ancient Christianity and the Olfactory Imagination*. Berkeley: University of California Press, 2006.

House, Ben. *Punic Wars and Culture Wars: Christian Essays on History and Teaching*. Nacogdoches, TX: Covenant Media Press, 2008.

Howes, David. "Foreword." In *The Varieties of Sensory Experience: A Sourcebook in the Anthropology of the Senses*, edited by David Howes. Toronto: University of Toronto Press, 1991.

Hübner, H. "ἀλήθεια." In *Exegetical Dictionary of the New Testament*, edited by Horst Balz et al., 1:57–60. Grand Rapids: Eerdmans, 1993.

Isidore of Seville. *Etymologies*. Translated by Stephen A. Barney et al. Cambridge: Cambridge University Press, 2006.

Jaeger, Werner. *Paideia: The Ideals of Greek Culture*. 3 vols. New York: Oxford University Press, 1944.

Johnson, Mark. *The Meaning of the Body: Aesthetics of Human Understanding*. Chicago: University of Chicago Press, 2012.

Jordan, James B. *Through New Eyes: Developing a Biblical View of the World.* Eugene, OR: Wipf & Stock, 1999.

Kittel, Gerhard et al., eds. *Theological Dictionary of the New Testament.* Translated by Geoffrey W. Bromiley. Grand Rapids: Eerdmans, 1977.

Kurtz, Paul. *The Making of Theatre History*. Englewood Cliffs, NJ: Prentice Hall, 1988.

Leder, Drew. *The Absent Body*. Chicago: University of Chicago Press, 1990.

Lee, Philip J. *Against the Protestant Gnostics*. New York: Oxford University Press, 1993.

Leithart, Peter J. *A House for My Name: A Survey of the Old Testament.* Moscow, ID: Canon, 2000.

Lewis, C. S. *The Abolition of Man or Reflections on Education with Special Reference to the Teaching of English in the Upper Forms of Schools*. New York: Harper & Row, 1971, 1974.

Lilley, Keith D. "Cities of God? Medieval Urban Forms and Their Christian Symbolism." *Transactions of the Institute of British Geographers*, New Series 29, no. 3 (September 2004): 296–313.

Long, Christopher P. *Aristotle on the Nature of Truth*. Cambridge: Cambridge University Press, 2010.

Longrigg, James. *Greek Rational Medicine: Philosophy and Medicine from Alcmaeon to the Alexandrians*. London: Routledge, 1993.

Louth, Andrew. "Later Theologians of the Greek East." In *The Early Christian World, Vol. 1*, edited by Philip F. Esler, 580–601. London: Routledge, 2000.

———. *Denys the Areopagite*. Wilton, CT: Morehouse-Barlow, 1989.

———. *Discerning the Mystery: An Essay on the Nature of Theology*. Oxford: Clarendon Press, 1983.

———. *The Origins of the Christian Mystical Tradition: From Plato to Denys*. Oxford: Oxford University Press, 1981.

———. "Theology, Contemplation and the University." *Studies in Christian Ethics* 17 (2004): 69–79.

Lundy, Miranda. "Sacred Number." In *Quadrivium: The Four Classical Liberal Arts of Number, Geometry, Music, and Cosmology*, edited by John Martineau, 7–56. New York: Walker and Company, 2010.

Lyon, M. L., and J. M. Barbalet. "Society's Body: Emotion and the 'Somatization' of Social Theory." In *Embodiment and Experience: The Existential Ground of Culture and Self*, edited by Thomas J. Csordas. Cambridge: Cambridge University Press, 1996.

Markos, Louis. *Restoring Beauty: The Good, the True, and the Beautiful in the Writings of C. S. Lewis*. Colorado Springs: Biblica, 2010.

McDonnell, Killian. *The Baptism of Jesus in the Jordan: The Trinitarian and Cosmic Order of Salvation*. Collegeville, MN: Liturgical Press, 1996.

McGrath, Alister E. *The Open Secret: A New Vision for Natural Theology*. Oxford: Blackwell Publishing, 2008.

McGuckin, John. "The Notion of the Beautiful in Ancient Greek Thought and Its Christian Patristic Transfiguration." *The Voice of Orthodoxy* XIII, no. 5 (September–October 2009). www.thevoiceoforthodoxy.com/archives/articles/notion_of_the_beautiful.html.

McGuire, Meredith B. "Religion and the Body: Rematerializing the Human Body in the Social Sciences of Religion." *Journal for the Scientific Study of Religion*. 29, no. 3 (1990): 283–96.

Nazianzus, Gregory. *Carmina* 2.1.1.180, cited in Margaret Barker, *Temple Themes in Christian Worship*. London: T&T Clark International, 2007.

Pépin, Jean. "Cosmic Piety." In *Classical Mediterranean Spirituality: Egyptian, Greek, Roman*, edited by A. H. Armstrong and A. A. Armstrong, 408–35. *World Spirituality* 15. New York: Crossroads, 1986.

Plato, *Cratylus, Parmenides, Greater Hippias, Lesser Hippias*. Edited and translated by Harold North Fowler. Loeb Classical Library. Cambridge: Harvard University Press, 1926.

———. *Laws*, Vol. II. Edited and translated by R.G. Bury. Loeb Classical Library. Cambridge: Harvard University Press, 1968.

———. *Phaedo*. Edited and translated by Harold North Fowler. *Plato* Vol. I. Loeb Classical Library. Cambridge: Harvard University Press, 1977.

———. *Theaetetus*. Edited and translated by H. N. Fowler. Loeb Classical Library. Cambridge: Harvard University Press, 1921.

———. *Timaeus*. Edited and translated by R.G. Bury. Loeb Classical Library. Cambridge: Harvard University Press, 1952.

Polanyi, Michael. *The Tacit Dimension*. New York: Doubleday, 1966.

Poythress, Vern S. *The Shadow of Christ in the Law of Moses*. Phillipsburg, NJ: P & R, 1995.

Ramos, Alice M. *Dynamic Transcendentals: Truth, Goodness, and Beauty from a Thomastic Perspective*. Washington, DC: Catholic University of America Press, 2012.

Rappaport, Roy A. *Ritual and Religion in the Making of Humanity*. Cambridge: Cambridge University Press, 1999.

Reyntiens, Patrick. "Art, Visual." In *The Oxford Companion to Christian Thought*, edited by Adrian Hastings et al. New York: Oxford University Press, 2000.

Rist, John. "On the Platonism of Gregory of Nyssa." *Hermathena* 169 (Winter 2000): 129–52.

Ruskin, John. *The Crown of Wild Olive: Three Lectures on Work, Traffic, and War*. New York: John Wiley & Sons, 1866.

Schindler, D. C. *Plato's Critique of Impure Reason: On Goodness and Truth in the Republic*. Baltimore: Catholic University of America Press, 2008.

Schmemann, Alexander. *Introduction to Liturgical Theology*. Crestwood, NY: St. Vladimir's Seminary Press, 1986.

Smith, James K. A. *Imagining the Kingdom: How Worship Works*. Grand Rapids: Baker Academic, 2013.

Solzhenitsyn, Aleksandr. "Beauty Will Save the World." The Nobel Lecture on Literature (1970), www.nobelprize.org/nobel_prizes/literature/laureates/1970/solzhenitsyn-lecture.html.

Sterling, Gregory E. "Prepositional Metaphysics in Jewish Wisdom Speculation and Early Christian Liturgical Texts." *Studia Philonica Annual* 9 (1997): 219–38.

Synnott, Anthony. "Puzzling over the Senses From Plato to Marx." In *The Variety of Sensory Experience*, edited by David Howes. Toronto: University of Toronto Press, 1991.

Townsend, Dabney. *Aesthetics: Classical Readings from the Western Tradition* 2nd ed. Belmont, CA: Wadsworth/Thomson Learning, 2001.

Viladesau, Richard. *Theological Aesthetics: God in Imagination, Beauty, and Art*. Oxford: Oxford University Press, 1999.

Wells, David F. *No Place for Truth: Or Whatever Happened to Evangelical Theology?* Grand Rapids: Eerdmans, 1994.

Wolfe, Gregory. *Beauty Will Save the World: Recovering the Human in an Ideological Age*. Wilmington, DE: Intercollegiate Studies Institute, 2011.

Wright, M. R. *Cosmology in Antiquity*. New York: Routledge, 1995.

Wright, N. T. "Paul's Gospel and Caesar's Empire." Center of Theological Inquiry public lecture. http://ntwrightpage.com/Wright_Paul_Caesar_Empire.pdf.

Young, Frances. *Biblical Exegesis and the Formation of Christian Culture*. Peabody, MA: Hendrickson, 1997.

About the Author

Steve Turley (PhD, Durham University) is a theologian, social theorist, classical Christian educator, and prize-winning classical guitarist. A faculty member at Tall Oaks Classical School in New Castle, Delaware, he teaches theology, Greek, and rhetoric. He is also Professor of Fine Arts at Eastern University. His research and writings have appeared in such journals as *Christianity and Literature*, *Calvin Theological Journal*, *First Things*, *Touchstone*, and *The Chesterton Review*. He and his wife, Akiko, have four children and live in Newark, DE, where together they enjoy fishing, gardening, and watching Duck Dynasty marathons.

Classical Education Book Series

An Introduction to Classical Education
A Guide for Parents

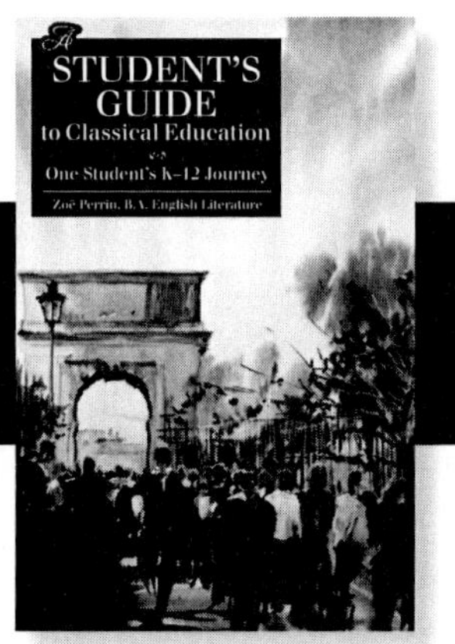

A Student's Guide to Classical Education
One Student's K–12 Journey

The Liberal Arts Tradition
A Philosophy of Christian Classical Education